INA CORINNE BROWN has been Professor of Anthropology at Scarritt College in the Nashville University Center since 1942. She has her Ph.D. in anthropology from the University of Chicago and has supplemented her studies by travel in Europe, Central Africa, India, and East Asia. Through teaching, writing, and lecturing, Dr. Brown has particularly endeavored to interpret anthropology to nonspecialists, both here and abroad.

For as one comes to understand people who live by institutions and values different from one's own, at the same time one comes to see that these people are, nevertheless, at bottom quite like one's own people. The alien culture at first appears to us as a mask, enigmatic or repugnant. On closer acquaintance we see it as a garment for the spirit; we understand its harmonies and appreciate them. Finally, as acquaintance goes deeper still, we do not see, or for a time forget, the culture, but look only to the common humanity of the men and women beneath.

ROBERT REDFIELD

"The Study of Culture in General Education," *Social Education*, Volume XI, No. 6, Oct. 1947, p. 262.

UNDERSTANDING
OTHER
CULTURES

INA CORINNE BROWN

Prentice-Hall, Inc., Englewood Cliffs, N.J. A SPECTRUM BOOK

© 1963 by PRENTICE-HALL, INC.
Englewood Cliffs, N.J.

*All rights reserved. No part of this book may be reproduced,
by mimeograph or any other means, without permission in
writing from the publishers.*

LIBRARY OF CONGRESS CATALOG NO.
63-9783

PRINTED IN THE UNITED STATES OF AMERICA
93616-C

Current printing (last digit):
17 16 15 14 13 12

FOREWORD

The notion that if people would just get to know one another they would be friends and everything would be all right is as dangerous as it is sentimental. Getting to know people is a necessary prelude to understanding and respect, but such knowledge alone will not resolve our differences or insure our liking people whose ways are alien to us. Persons may know one another very well and yet be bitter rivals and equally bitter enemies. Nor does a common race, religion, language, nationality, or culture insure friendliness or good will as numerous civil wars, rebellions, and intergroup conflicts attest. The sober truth is that different peoples must learn to get along together whether they like one another or not.

No matter how different other peoples may seem, their ways are not peculiar, unnatural, or incomprehensible. The more we know of other cultures the more evident it becomes that no society could hold together unless its patterns of thinking, feeling, and acting were reasonably systematic and coherent. The first principle of anthropology is that cultures must be studied as wholes, and no custom or belief can be properly understood unless seen in the context within which it operates. To understand other peoples, then, we must have some idea of what culture is and how it functions and some knowledge of the variety of ways in which different human groups have gone about solving universal problems.

There was a time when an understanding of other peoples was important mainly to diplomats, military personnel, missionaries, and businessmen with overseas interests. Today, the various cultures of the world are everybody's business, and the behavior of almost any individual may have important ramifications in world affairs. People now take vacations in distant and formerly inaccessible places, and enormous numbers of Americans go abroad to live and work. Thousands of persons from other cultures come to this country each year, many of them students who return home to become leaders in their own countries. The day-to-day experience of these persons with ordinary Americans is likely to determine whether we part with feelings of warmth or of animosity for one another.

This book is written primarily for the general reader who has no background in anthropology. It is not intended as a formal text, but I hope it will be useful as a means of adding a broader cultural dimension to beginning college courses in the social sciences, education, and related fields. I hope it may be useful also to public school teachers and others who have the responsibility of helping to prepare the oncoming generation for planetary, if not interplanetary, living.

I have tried to be as objective as possible but, as someone has expressed it, man is a value-creating animal, and to deny that one has values is to proclaim oneself as less than fully human. I make no apologies, therefore, for the fact that this volume is value-oriented in the sense that it reflects a concern for the furtherance of what has been called the human use of human beings.

The reader who is not concerned with sources may read through the book without being interrupted by footnotes. Those who would like to know the sources of information or who wish some guidance for further reading will find notes, references, and a bibliography at the end of the volume.

I am indebted to the teachers under whom I received my training in anthropology at the University of Chicago, and to my fellow anthropologists, whose researches have created a common pool of knowledge about other peoples. The authors on whose books I have drawn most heavily for material are referred to in the *Notes and References* and in the *Bibliography*. My debt is less specific, but no less great, to the numerous other persons whose publications could not be cited for want of space.

I am indebted also to my students in the Nashville University Center who have taught me many things. I am particularly grateful to the students from other parts of the world whose presence in my classes always gives new dimensions to the content of any course

I.C.B.

Scarritt College
Nashville, Tennessee

CONTENTS

*It makes little difference whether the penguins of Antarctica
know anything about the squirrels of Rock Creek Park. But it
makes all the difference in the world whether the American
people understand the crowded millions who inhabit Asia.
Your destiny, Asia's destiny, the world's very survival, may
depend on such an understanding on your part.*

CARLOS P. ROMULO*

1. MAN AND CULTURE

1. To Each His Own

A few years ago a Walt Disney movie pictured a Through-the-Looking-Glass land in which trains stood still while the stations moved up and down the tracks, horses rode the jockeys in the races, houses caught on water and were put out by fire, and the stork brought parents to babies. It was a delightful bit of nonsense.

Westerners who go into other countries sometimes feel as if they were in some such topsy-turvy situation. Aside from any difference in physical type there is a sense of strangeness about everything. The speech seems rapid and unintelligible; gestures and facial expressions are strange; dress and ornamentation are peculiar; houses, furniture, and utensils appear odd. The food may seem tasteless or be too highly seasoned. Various behavior patterns may seem not only queer but wrong or unnatural. Any effort to find out why people behave in these seemingly queer ways rarely brings a satisfactory answer. People usually do not know why they act as they do except that they have always done it that way.

There is nothing unusual about such inability to give reasons for accepted forms of behavior. After all, an American asked why he calls the brothers of his parents and the husbands of his parents' sisters by the same kinship term, is likely to reply, "Because they are all uncles," or he may ask, "What else could you call them?" Were he asked why he doesn't eat fruit salad or ice cream and cake

* *The Asian Student,* January 27, 1957.

for breakfast, his reply would likely be, that they wouldn't be good, or that nobody does it, or that they aren't suitable breakfast foods. It is doubtful if he could make a Greenland Eskimo or a South Sea Islander understand how cold fruit juice, fresh fruits, boiled eggs, cereals with cream and sugar, or waffles with honey are particularly different from fruit salad, ice cream, and cake. If it isn't the cold or the sweet, the fruit or the eggs, the cream or the flour—all of which we find acceptable for breakfast in other forms—then what is it? The simple fact is that people usually think, feel, and act as they do because they were brought up in a culture in which these ways were accepted, not only as good and right, but as natural.

Many social patterns, customs, or folkways—whatever we choose to call them—are not inherently right or wrong, but they are important because their observance by everybody makes large areas of life predictable. Without them we would not know what to expect of other people or what they might be expecting of us. Furthermore, little would ever get done if we had to decide each time on procedure for these now patterned ways. Such patterns are like traffic laws: it doesn't really matter whether people drive to the left as in Britain or to the right as in the United States, but it becomes a matter of life and death that all drivers in any given place follow the same rules. When patterns involve basic values important to the society's well-being, they get into the category of what people think of as right and wrong.

Westerners are sometimes surprised to discover that many other peoples not only regard their own ways as right but may consider themselves superior to the rest of the world. The notion that "We are the people" is an old one. Back in the fifth century B.C. Herodotus said he was sure the Persian king must be mad because no one in his right mind would go about mocking other people's long established customs as Cambyses had done. "For," said Herodotus, "if one were to offer men the choice of all the customs in the world, they would examine the whole number and end up by preferring their own."

Many of the more isolated peoples of the world refer to themselves by terms that mean men or human beings. When Europeans first met Carib Indians, the Caribs announced that "we alone are people." The Hottentots' name for themselves meant men of men. Numerous other groups in Africa, aboriginal America, and elsewhere called themselves by terms that translate the wealthy ones, the intelligible ones, or, as the Navaho, simply people. The Greenland Eskimos thought the Europeans who arrived on their shores had come to learn virtue and good manners from their hosts. Numerous tribal peoples living in places that struck Europeans as particularly desolate were not only content with themselves but felt they lived in the best of all possible worlds.

The view that one's own country is the center of everything and that all others may be scaled or rated with reference to it is generally recognized as being associated with the integration and solidarity of the group. When not carried too far this ethnocentric attitude serves a useful purpose in that the very existence of a society depends on a fairly high degree of consensus. An orderly society is possible only so long as a considerable number of its members believe that their own particular habits and customs are right and proper and therefore, presumably, superior. So long as most peoples lived in relatively small and isolated groups such attitudes were not a serious threat to other societies. Today, however, the peoples of the world are so bound together that survival on our planet depends on knowledge and understanding of one another and respect for peoples whose ways are different from one's own.

Understanding the ways of other peoples is important also because such understanding increases our own self-knowledge and objectivity. We grow up with the assumption that our own way of doing things is the right way, if not the only way. Yet we are aware of many problems for which we do not know the solutions. A knowledge of the variety of ways in which other peoples have met similar problems gives us new perspectives and new clues to human behavior. "He knows not England who only England knows" applies equally to any society.

2. Culture and Society

In its popular use the word culture usually refers to refinement or cultivation. The cultured person is thought to be one who is well educated, well mannered, and refined in behavior; who appreciates a certain type of art and prefers Beethoven to the latest hit tunes. As used in this book culture has a different and more specialized meaning. It refers to all the accepted and patterned ways of behavior of a given people. It is a body of common understandings. It is the sum total and the organization or arrangement of all the group's ways of thinking, feeling, and acting. It also includes the physical manifestations of the group as exhibited in the objects they make—the clothing, shelter, tools, weapons, implements, uten-sils, and so on. In this sense, of course, every people—however primitive—has a culture, and no individual can live without cul-ture.

It is our culture that enables us to get through the day because both we and the other people we encounter attach somewhat the same meanings to the same things. Our culture is our routine of sleeping, bathing, dressing, eating, and getting to work. It is our household chores and the actions we perform on the job; the way we buy goods and services, write and mail a letter, take a taxi or board a bus, make a telephone call, go to a movie, or attend church. It is the way we greet friends or address a stranger, the admonitions we give our children and the way they respond, what we consider good and bad manners, and even to a large extent what we con-sider right and wrong. All these and thousands of other ways of thinking, feeling, and acting seem so natural and right that we may even wonder how else one could do it. But to millions of other people in the world every one of these acts would seem strange, awkward, incomprehensible, unnatural, or wrong. These people would perform many, if not all, of the same acts, but they would be done in different ways that to them would seem logical, natural, and right.

There are various approaches we can make to culture. We can look at it descriptively, that is, simply describe what it looks like, the form it takes. We can, for example, talk about the differences in material culture by describing the different tools used in getting food. We can compare the digging stick—a sharp pointed stick used for digging up roots and plants for food—with the short-handled hoe, the plow, or the complicated tractors, threshers, reapers, and binders, used in modern mechanized agriculture. Or we can talk about forks versus chopsticks (or fingers), or mats or hammocks versus beds, or moccasins, straw sandals and leather shoes, or bows and arrows, swords, spears, guns, cannon, or atomic bombs and guided missiles. All of these things represent different ways in which people have developed certain material objects which are used as means to certain ends. But in each case the material object repre-sents an idea, not only an accepted way of making an object but an accepted conception of its use.

We can look at other aspects of culture in the same way. We can look at certain institutions that are found everywhere, such as mar-riage, and say that one society is monogamous while another allows polygamy, though the specialist will use different terms if he means plural wives or plural husbands. We can also talk about different patterns of classifying relatives, performing the marriage ceremony, handling a corpse, or approaching the gods or spirits.

But these descriptions do not in themselves help us to understand other peoples. We could compile a whole book of such descriptions and come out with the idea merely that other people are a queer lot who have never learned the right way to do things. A culture consists not only of elements or traits but also of their interrelationships and organization. Two buildings may consist of the same number of bricks of the same shape and size, put together by the same amount of mortar, and yet bear little resemblance to one another either in structure or function. Different cultures may have many specific patterns that are similar, but within each culture there is an organization or configuration that makes of it an integrated whole. This fact suggests at once that a change in one part of the culture affects all other parts.

The most profitable way to look at culture is to see it as an adaptive mechanism, that is, to see what it does. In this sense a culture is a body of ready-made solutions to the problems encountered by the group. It is, as someone has put it, a cushion between man and his environment. In order to meet their needs, people must devise ways of dealing with their environment so as to get food, clothing, and shelter. They must establish and maintain certain patterns of relationships, for in each society there will be males and females, infants, growing children, youths, adults, and the aged. They must care for the children and train them in the ways of the society so they may take their places as responsible members of the group. They must find ways to maintain the cohesion of the group and preserve consensus. In all societies the members must come to have strong sentiments about various ideas, purposes, and goals—the things we call values. And if men are to be willing to live by the society's rules, they must have some outlet for the expression of self and some way of relating to the forces outside themselves. No society limits itself to the strictly utilitarian. In all of them there is some form of art, music, dance, song, or story, and there are rites and ceremonies which, in the broadest sense of the word, we may call religious.

The resulting culture has form and pattern. There is a degree of order and system that gives to the people who participate in it a certain style of life that is peculiarly their own. It is not that the people sit down together and consciously plan these things. Most people accept their culture as "given" and usually they are not aware of why they do things in a particular way.

It is easy to see why there are fundamental likenesses in all cultures when we remember that all human organisms are essentially alike and that, by virtue of this fact, man's basic needs are the same. Moreover, man has essentially the same resources and the same cues offered by nature though, of course, these vary in specific ways. Everywhere man is dependent on land, water, minerals, plants, and animals. Everywhere he deals with climate and weather. Everywhere he has before him the forms, colors, and textures offered by nature. There is almost everywhere some sort of seasonal cycle of warm and cold, or wet and dry, and there is the day and the night. There is the life cycle of plants and animals. There is the human organism itself, male and female, and the developmental sequence from infancy to old age. And, finally, there is over him and around him the mystery of birth and death, of sleeping and waking, of dreams, of sickness and health, of the changing seasons, the sun and the moon and the stars. All of these and more offer to peoples the clues and the cues they need and use to build their cultures. No people uses them all and no two groups use them in exactly the same way. And so our cultures are alike in many ways, different in others.

The terms culture and society are frequently used interchangeably, and there is usually no great harm in doing so as long as we know what the difference is. In simplest form, we can say that a society is always made up of people; their culture is the way they behave. In other words, a society is not a culture; it has a culture. In one sense a society is any kind of associational group that has some degree of permanence. In this sense churches and clubs are societies and we speak of a debating society or a medical society. In the anthropological sense a society is a more or less permanent, relatively large, relatively stable, aggregate of people who live and work together, and who share a common body of meanings and a common system of values. It is this type of aggregate that we mean when we speak of *our society, Japanese society* or *Crow Indian society.*

Although we can say that each society has a culture, it does not follow that there are no cultural differences within a given society or that several different societies may not share, at least to a large extent, a common culture. As a geopolitical unit, the United States constitutes one society yet, even if we exclude groups like the American Indians or the foreign born, there is considerable variation in culture patterns within the continental United States. On the other hand, we share to a large extent a common culture with Canada, a separate, well-defined society that forms an independent political unit.

Some writers have used the term The Great Society to refer to civilization as a whole. Others have used civilization in contrast with the term culture. In this book, culture will be used as an inclusive term referring to the patterned ways of all peoples, however simple or complex their life may be. Civilization will be used only when we need to distinguish a certain kind of culture, usually a fairly sophisticated one that uses writing, has an urban life, and a complex economic and political organization. Civilization, then, is not "better than" but only more complex in certain ways than other types of culture.

We are, however, still confronted with the problem of distinguishing various cultures and societies by their degrees of complexity. The term *savages,* once used to refer to the peoples who were not considered "civilized," now sounds strange to our ears. The word *primitive* is still commonly used even by anthropologists, who refer to primitive society, primitive culture, primitive art and primitive religion, and various peoples are still referred to as primitives. But anthropologists are not happy with the word primitive used in this way, and "the primitives" probably won't be happy with it either when they find out about it. The term came into use at a time when it was commonly assumed that the way the so-called primitives live today represented the way "early man" was supposed to have lived. Now we know that the way of life of people in even the simplest culture today does not represent a form of arrested development. Moreover, the term has another disadvantage in that it carries the implication that such societies, or cultures, are all alike and this, of course, is not true.

Various other terms have been suggested, such as *simple, preliterate, nonliterate,* and *small scale,* but none of these designations is wholly satisfactory. In this book the word *primitive* has been avoided except in a few instances when nothing else seemed to fit. Most of the other common terms are used interchangeably, but always with an unspoken apology to the peoples who deserve a more suitable designation.

3. Other Aspects of Culture

Religion, nationality, and language are aspects of culture that often set peoples apart from one another. In simple societies religion is usually coextensive with the political or tribal unit; in more complex societies many different religions may be represented in the same culture. Religion will be treated more fully in a later section; mention is made of it here to emphasize the fact that religion is always a part of one's learned behavior and is therefore a part of culture, not an aspect of race.

Nationality is an elusive term that is used in a variety of ways. It is often used as if it implied either religious or linguistic unity, sometimes both, though neither is necessarily involved. Many people believe that both language and religion are natural expressions of the people of a given race and that racial identity is inherent in nationality. There are, however, people of the same race who are clearly of different nationalities and other people may feel a sense of national unity though they are of different races. Brazil is a multiracial nation whose citizens feel a strong sense of national identity. India is a nation of different religions, and there is no single Indian language that is understood by everybody, yet most of the people of India feel strongly that they share a common nationality.

Language is an aspect of culture, yet people speaking different languages may share a common culture. On the other hand, a language may extend beyond national and cultural boundaries, though usually not without some modification. In the sense of being able fully to communicate with one another, most of the people of England, Australia, Canada and the United States speak the same language; in reality there are a considerable number of variations as any American visitor to England or Australia has discovered.

When they first encountered peoples with entirely different languages Europeans assumed that the forms of Latin grammar were universal categories inherent in the nature of reality. As a consequence all kinds of languages were forced into what someone has described as the procrustean bed of parts of speech, gender, case, number, tense, voice, and mode. When a given language did not lend itself to these particular categories it was thought to be rude, uncultivated and "primitive." As anthropologists made studies of other cultures and other languages it became apparent that the categories of classical grammar were neither absolute nor universal. It was seen that language is not merely a means of communication but also a special way of looking at the world and of organizing experience and that the pie of experience can be sliced in many different ways. Today the knowledgeable student of languages avoids imposing patterns from the outside and tries instead to discover the categories inherent in each particular language.

Many people have the notion that "primitive" peoples speak "primitive" languages that are simple in structure and limited in vocabulary. The facts are otherwise. Many of the unwritten languages of the world are extremely complex with vocabularies that are full and precise with reference to aspects of the culture that are important to the people. The Navaho, for example, are reported to have more than a thousand recorded names for plants and hundreds of terms used in referring to ceremonies or to specialized occupations. Eskimos have many different words for different kinds of snow.

Languages vary in the things to which they give emphasis as well as in specialized terms. In English one plural is used whether we mean two things or two thousand, whether they are all together or separate, present or absent. "We" may mean you and me, all of a group to which I belong, or me and one or more persons who are not present. "You" may mean anything from one person to thousands. There are other languages that have one plural for things bunched together and another meaning things scattered about. There are languages that have a "we" meaning you and me only and another "we" that includes other people. There are languages in which there are separate terms used for things present and for things absent.

In English one can say "I went to town" without indicating the means used to get there. The Navaho would have no equivalent of the general "went" but would need to specify whether he walked, rode a horse, rode in a wagon, a car, a train or a plane. On the other hand there are things you cannot be general about in English unless you use extra words in which to do it. In some pronouns we have to indicate sex just as the Navaho had to indicate the means by which he went. When we cannot or do not wish to identify the sex of the person referred to, we either have to use "he" as being inclusive of "she" or we use the awkward "he or she," or, in many cases, we fall back on an incorrect plural and say "they" although one person is meant.

Every language involves a particular system of sounds to which meanings are attached, and speakers of the language learn to produce these sounds and to recognize them when they are used by other people. It is difficult for an adult to learn to speak or even to hear the significant differences in another speech system. Many Chinese and Japanese who learn English as adults simply do not hear our *l* and *r* as distinct sounds. On the other hand, most Indo-European speakers find the tone languages spoken in China, in Africa and elsewhere in the world extremely difficult. Since such tones are not significant sounds in Indo-European languages we find it difficult either to hear or to repeat them even when they are called to our attention.

Among many African languages the use of a high, middle, or low tone may not only modify but may completely change the meaning of a word. When the words of an African tone language are set to Western music, as is frequently done with hymns and songs used in Western-directed churches and schools, the meaning of the words may be so distorted by the accent and tone imposed by the music that the songs become either unintelligible to the African or completely changed in meaning. Yet many Westerners have lived for years among African peoples without "hearing" these tones as significant sounds.

While it is difficult for most adults to learn to speak a foreign language perfectly, that is, without an accent, a child readily learns as its "native" language the one it hears spoken by the people around it as it first learns to speak. Any normal human being can easily learn to speak "like a native" any language he hears from infancy.

4. Race and Culture

Religion, nationality, and language are a part of our social, not our biological, heritage. We "inherit" these social and cultural patterns in the sense that we inherit lands or property and not as we inherit the genes that account for our brown or blue eyes, our straight or curly hair, or our fair or dark skins. The basic physical characteristics that are used in setting up racial categories come to us through the mechanism of biological inheritance and they are determined by the genetic make-up of our parents and the family lines they represent. Race thus stands apart from culture in that racial characteristics are physical and inborn, not learned or acquired by the individual after birth. A person's race thus tells us nothing at all about his religion, his nationality, his language or his manners and morals. There is no French race, no Irish, Latin, Anglo-Saxon, Aryan, or Jewish races. These terms properly refer to nationalities, languages, socioreligious groups or what are sometimes called ethnic groups. Nobody knows what the original Aryan speakers looked like and the Jews of the world include almost every known physical type. Jews are thus a socioreligious group, not a race in the proper meaning of the term.

There is no definition of race that is wholly satisfactory even when we attach a long string of conditions to it. For our purposes here we can say that a race is a population having in common a combination of inherited physical characteristics that set it apart from other populations having other combinations of such physical characteristics.

But whatever definition we use there is no way by which the peoples of the world can be divided into neat, precise, and orderly racial categories. Most anthropologists agree on the broad divisions of Caucasoid, Mongoloid, and Negroid with Australoids sometimes making a fourth division. But there are wide variations within these groupings and there are many peoples of the world who do not fit into any of these categories. Moreover, peoples of different physical types have mixed with one another since the beginning of recorded history and doubtless before that time. There is therefore no clear-cut and simple way by which peoples everywhere can be placed into specific racial categories with specific characteristics.

Most of the criteria used by anthropologists in determining racial categories have to do with physical characteristics that are of little or no consequence in human behavior except as they are made so by the way people feel about them. Skin color and certain other physical characteristics may be advantageous or disadvantageous in given environments but there is no evidence that skin color, hair, or other such features are in any way correlated with a particular kind of brain or with special qualities of mind and character. Moreover, recent studies by physical anthropologists indicate that the genes responsible for different characteristics not only may be inherited independently of one another but that the physical characteristics of a population may change over a period of time even when there has been no admixture with other races.

There is no evidence that the people of any one race are innately superior or inferior in general mental ability to the peoples of other races. Unquestionably individuals come into the world with different potentialities but the evidence suggests that within any of the major racial groups the whole range of individual potentialities will be found. This does not necessarily mean that there are no statistically significant differences in specific innate abilities occurring in widely separated populations. It does mean that we do not now have any reliable way of determining whether such differences exist. Furthermore a given people might conceivably be superior in one way but inferior in another. Even if it were possible to determine that in some population there was a greater than average incidence of one kind of ability or another we would still have to reckon with the various cultural factors involved. We would also be confronted with the fact that there are no objective criteria for deciding the relative superiority of mechanical aptitude, literary or artistic gifts, philosophical bent, and so on.

There are not now and probably never were any "pure" races and there is no evidence that serious biological evils result from race mixture as such. Most of the problems that arise from such mixture grow out of the way in which people think and feel about it, that is, the problems are social not biological.

It is important to note that however we define race or whatever classifications we make, human beings are more alike than they are different. It is generally accepted by most scientists that present day human beings all belong to the same species and people of the most diverse types have interbred freely when brought into contact. In fact, if people of different races had the natural antipathy sometimes attributed to them there would be no need either of laws or the threat of social penalties to keep them apart.

Although there is no evidence that the biological fact of race in any way determines culture, what people think about race and the way they feel about their own and other races are a part of their learned behavior and in this sense are aspects of culture. People in different cultures may define race in quite different ways and they may feel very strongly about their definitions.

It should be noted also that different peoples use different criteria in classifying the peoples of mixed racial ancestry. In the United States we classify as a Negro any person who looks like a Negro, who is known to have had a Negro ancestor, or who admits to having had such an ancestor. Actually, a number of these persons are biologically more white than Negro so that our definition is in part at least a legal and social rather than a biological one.

In other parts of the world people may define race quite differently. In most Latin American countries having considerable Negro and Indian populations persons are classified on the basis of culture rather than of race. There is a Brazilian saying that a rich Negro is a white man and a poor white man is a Negro. This does not mean that the biological facts of race are completely ignored, but economic and cultural factors enter into their interpretations. In most of Latin America an Indian is a person with Indian culture. Two brothers may be regarded one as white and the other as Indian, or a person may "become white" if he learns to talk, dress, and act according to European rather than Indian custom. These patterns vary somewhat from one Latin American country to another, but nowhere in Latin America is there the kind of segregation widely practiced in the United States, and nowhere is one's race defined on the basis of a single ancestor.

Just as most peoples seem to prefer their own culture so do most of them seem to prefer their own physical type. The people in one New Guinea tribe still refer to white people by a term that can only be translated as "monstrous" or "unnatural." Another tribe assumed that Europeans wore clothes because they were ashamed of their white skins. Among some African peoples the original idea of beauty was a jet black skin, and in one tribe it was believed that white skins were a curse that God placed on Europeans because one of their ancestors had committed incest with his mother.

The common preference for one's own physical type is illustrated in a creation myth reported from the Malay people. The Creator made the first man of clay and baked him in the oven but took him out too soon. He had a very unattractive pasty white skin and lanky hair. He became the ancestor of the white people. The Creator tried again but this time he left the man in too long. His skin was burned black and his hair frizzled by the heat. This one became the ancestor of the Negroes. Profiting by his earlier mistakes, the Creator got the third one just right, a beautiful golden brown. This one, needless to say, became the ancestor of the Malays who look just as men should.

Although preference for one's own physical type seems to have been usual, race prejudice such as we know it seems not to have existed in the civilized world until after the rise of the African slave trade to the West. There was group antipathy which those who "read history backwards" sometimes take to be race prejudice but the physical differences of race or color appear not to have been the major factors. The extreme color consciousness in the world today seems to be a special development related to such factors as slavery and European colonial expansion which resulted in the political and economic subordination of many of the world's darker peoples.

These facts are relevant to our world situation today for we are prone to assume that it is race itself that underlies our differences. The evidence, however, all points to the fact that it is not race itself, but the way in which we think, feel, and act about real or assumed biological differences that is important in our relationships with other peoples. If we are to understand other peoples we must interpret culture in cultural terms. All sorts of cultures have been produced by peoples of the same race and of different races, and the normal members of any race seem perfectly capable of normal participation in any culture into which they are born or into which they are taken as infants. Race as such then has nothing to do with nationality, language, religion, or with cultural creativity.

5. In Search of Understanding

It is difficult, perhaps impossible, for any person ever fully to "get inside" a culture that is not his own. There are, however, certain approaches, points of view, techniques, and procedures by which one can gain insight and a measure of understanding. The later chapters of this book are in large measure given to a discussion of the variety of ways in which human groups have met their problems. These accounts will have more meaning if we first look at some of the more fruitful ways in which one may approach the study of other cultures.

Any people's social heritage is to them what "The American Way," in its best sense, is to us. It is the Pilgrim Fathers and Thanksgiving Day, the Boston Tea Party and the Fourth of July; George Washington and a cherry tree, Abraham Lincoln and a log cabin. It is Santa Claus and a manger, Easter lilies and Easter rabbits, the flag, Coney Island, camp meetings, Sunday dinner, fried chicken, ice cream and apple pie. It is Yankee Doodle, Tipperary, and My Old Kentucky Home. It is a thousand and one things, sublime and ridiculous, good and bad, mythical and real, that make us a people and not merely an aggregate of individuals whose ancestors came from just about everywhere. Many of these patterns have come to us from other peoples but we have made them peculiarly our own.

It is a common social heritage that makes for cohesion and solidarity and that thus helps insure the continuity of group life. It is in this heritage that each new generation finds its value system and a faith to live by. People can and do modify and change their social patterns but when whole peoples are ruthlessly separated from their past the result is almost always disorganization and deterioration. We have seen this cultural breakdown in peoples who somehow seemed to lose the will to live and who literally died out under the impact of a conquest that took all the meaning out of life. We have seen it in the pathetic deterioration of many once proud Indian tribes whose cup of life was broken under the impact of the white man. We have seen it, too, in American Negroes, robbed of their African heritage and prevented from accepting in full the new heritage that was being forged as a part of the American dream. We are seeing it today take a new form as totalitarian governments consciously and ruthlessly go about making other peoples over in their own image.

In insisting that cultures must be studied as wholes we are really saying that no custom, belief, or behavior can be understood out of its social or cultural context. That is, any item of behavior, any tradition or pattern, can be evaluated correctly only in the light of its meaning to the people who practice it, its relation to other elements of the culture, and the part it plays in the adaptation of the people to their environment or to one another. No custom is "odd" to the people who practice it.

The specialist who goes into another culture sees the unusual things but he looks for the regularities and the way basic problems are met. He observes not merely the overt behavior but seeks to get at the underlying premises on which such behavior rests. Many administrators and missionaries have struggled in vain to change some custom because they did not understand that they and the people they were trying to help were operating from different sets of presuppositions. Moreover, any given act of behavior may seem familiar but may have an entirely different meaning from that of a similar pattern in one's own culture.

Persons going into other cultures as government employees or missionaries are often given what has come to be called "area orientation," a program in which they are briefed on the customs of the country. This procedure has its value but far more valuable is a point of view, an understanding of what culture is and what it does, and some knowledge of the variety of ways in which human behavior has been institutionalized. This theoretical knowledge of culture gives clues and cues to the behavior of human groups wherever they are found.

One of the problems encountered in writing such a book as this is the use of the present and the past tense. Anthropologists writing about the simple societies they study usually use what is known as the ethnological present. That is, they write in the present tense as if the situation were now as it was at the time they saw it or even as some old man remembered it. In the past the peoples described were usually nonliterate and were not likely to be self-conscious about their "progress." Today in many of these societies there is an educated and self-conscious elite who want the world to know that times have changed with them as with other peoples. For the purposes of this book it is not important whether a particular pattern still exists in the form in which it was first reported. It *is* important that the reader recognize that times are changing in even the more isolated parts of the world. Therefore, in most cases when referring to specific peoples I have used what may be called the ethnological past. In any case, the world is changing so rapidly that the old and new often exist side by side and a custom that is practiced as I write may have been superseded before this book is in print.

To get the whole world out of bed
And washed, and dressed, and warmed, and fed,
To work, and back to bed again,
Believe me, Saul, costs worlds of pain

JOHN MASEFIELD*

2. THE WORK OF THE WORLD

1. Who Does What

Human groups everywhere are faced with the same basic problems of physical survival: they must discover ways to meet the elementary needs of food, clothing, and shelter, and they must protect themselves from the onslaughts of their natural environment or from animals or human enemies who may threaten them or their means of livelihood.

It is difficult for most of the persons who live in modern industrial societies to comprehend the struggle for mere existence that even today confronts many of the peoples of the world. In a modern urban society located in a favorable region the majority of people may live out their lives without ever having been threatened with uncontrolled natural forces. In fact, the average urban dweller of the Western world is so many times removed from direct contact with his natural environment that he is scarcely aware of its existence, much less of its importance to him. Our foods are packaged, canned, frozen, and often pre-cooked or ready to serve, and our clothing is likely to come to us ready made. Even the responsibility of heating our houses is increasingly a matter of adjusting a thermostat. In spite of the popular interest in do-it-yourself projects, if we are modern urban dwellers we are insulated from our environment by an array of gadgets and an army of professionals who serve as middlemen between us and the source of supplies on which all human lives depend.

* "The Everlasting Mercy" from *The Poems and Plays of John Masefield*, Vol. I (New York: The Macmillan Company, 1920). Reprinted by permission of The Macmillan Company.

It is otherwise with the many peoples of the world who must deal more directly with the land or the sea. To many peoples eating meat means killing and dressing domestic animals, wild game, or fish which they have raised, hunted or caught. Vegetable foods come to them as a result of their labors in gardens, field, or forest, and such products must often be shucked, pounded, ground, or otherwise laboriously treated before they can be cooked and eaten. Most of the peoples of the world can now buy cloth, but the garments may still have to be cut and sewed at home. Houses in many parts of the world still require the cutting of trees or the making of bricks or thatch by local labor. In many of the simpler cultures firewood is still brought daily from the forest and water from a stream or the village well. Moreover, in many areas of the world people must wrestle with extremes of heat or cold, with droughts or floods and sometimes with both in the course of a single year. They may have to cope with poor soil or dense jungle growth. They may live in areas where domestic animals cannot be kept or where parasites, insects, and predatory animals threaten health and life.

Nowhere does the natural environment completely determine the ways of men but everywhere it limits and influences the human condition. Locally available resources may be bountiful and constant, or scanty and variable but until the development of industry, trade, and wide scale communication, a large proportion of the world's peoples were dependent on local supplies, and on their own and their neighbor's skills in securing them. Simple hunting and gathering economies dependent on wild plants and animals survive in only a few places in the world today but many peoples in less developed areas still depend for their food on garden culture, the keeping of flocks and herds, or on a subsistence agriculture that may combine the two. Many such peoples also gather wild fruits, berries, nuts, and plants, and they may hunt and fish to add to their food supply.

Whatever his environment man cannot provide his food, clothe or shelter his body, or protect himself from enemies with his bare hands. He has no powerful jaws or teeth, no claws or horns or hooves, to use in getting food or in attacking enemies, and he lacks the natural body covering of hair, fur, or feathers that protects the nonhuman creatures. If he is to survive he must use his brain, his remarkably versatile hands, his stereoscopic vision, and his upright position to provide himself with what has sometimes been called a third hand. In even the simplest cultures, man has devised extensions of his body in the form of tools, weapons, implements, and utensils with which he manipulates his environment so that it better meets his needs. He has built himself shelters, and covered his body to provide a portable shelter. He has domesticated plants and taught animals to serve his needs, and he has learned to trade with his neighbors for things that his local habitat could not supply.

In every society there must be some sort of patterned ways of behaving that are understood and observed by everybody. There must be some kind of accepted division of labor, to determine who shall do what, and there must be an agreement about each person's rights and duties with reference to every other member of the group. If the group is to perpetuate itself, women must bear children and a reasonable number of the children must survive their period of helplessness and dependence. In practically all simple societies all women marry as soon as they are physiologically mature, and child bearing is their expected role. In such societies an infant usually can survive only if fed at the human breast, and people are rarely well enough nourished for a woman to provide food for more than one child at a time. Where there is no milk or other food especially suitable for infants a child may be breast fed for two or three years. Under such circumstances women are more often than not physically handicapped as far as speed and general mobility are concerned because, for much of the time, they are either heavy with child or have a young child dependent on their physical presence for food. It is not that such women do not work hard; in some societies they may be veritable beasts of burden. But they are not in a position to be hunters, warriors, or herders of flocks that must be taken to distant pastures or guarded day and night.

In the majority of societies men do all the fighting, and at least most of the hunting. Almost everywhere women keep house, prepare food, and care for young children. But beyond this point generalizations are studded with exceptions. Other than bearing children and feeding them at the breast, there is no task that everywhere in the world is considered exclusively woman's work. There are many societies in which trapping small animals, fishing, and gardening or hoe culture are commonly left to women, though there are a number of societies in which husbands and wives share the garden work or have separate gardens, each tending his own. Herding is most often done by men or boys, but milking in some societies is a man's job, in others it is woman's work, and in still others it may be done by either men or women. Although men most often set up the framework for houses, the women sometimes do the thatching, and frequently it is the women who plaster the walls and floors. The care of the house usually falls to women. The dressing of skins, weaving, and the making of garments are sometimes men's work, sometimes women's work, and sometimes the work of both.

It is out of the necessities of physical survival and out of the need for the care of children that there has grown up everywhere a division of labor between the sexes, carried out largely within the cooperative institution we know as the family. To be sure, the family satisfies other needs—for a sexual partner, companionship, and so on. But, with the exception of economic cooperation and the care of young children, almost every need which the family meets in one society may be met in some other way in another society. Our own modern concept of the wife as many women—wife, mother, household manager, hostess, companion to husband and to children, perhaps church and community leader, and glamor girl in the bargain—is utterly alien to much of the rest of the world. In many areas of the world husbands and wives never attend social affairs together nor do they together entertain guests in their home. But almost everywhere they cooperate in the meeting of the physical needs of themselves and their children, and everywhere there are some tasks that men normally do and others which fall to the lot of women.

In our own society the roles of men and women have varied with time, circumstances, and economic levels. Pioneer women worked side by side with their men and either of them handled guns and plows or drove oxen as the need dictated. Today women in our society may be found in most of the occupations open to men, but their numbers are few in both top executive positions and in jobs requiring brawn or exposure to rough conditions. Preparation of food, cooking, sewing, cleaning, and similar household tasks are still woman's work in the eyes of most Americans. Yet almost all these tasks are done by men too when performed outside the home. The chef, the waiter, the dishwasher, the Pullman porter, the tailor, and even the designers of women's dresses and hats are more often than not males.

In the simplest societies, the division of labor is on a sex-age basis. Boys learn how to do men's work from their fathers or other male relatives, and girls learn women's work by assisting their

mothers. Often, specific tasks are assigned children at certain ages—
for example, in some South African tribes young boys herd goats,
but are trusted with the cattle only after the initiation ceremonies
by which they are promoted to the status of men.

So long as there is this simple sex-age division of labor with only
limited specialization, the relationships of most people are determined by their kin group. When people begin to specialize, associational groups come into being. In the simple society this may
be a group of age mates who are warriors, a club of men who have
achieved certain economic goals, or some sort of craft guild. The
specialists most commonly found are the metal worker and the
diviner, priest, or shaman, but there may also be persons whose
skill in making pottery, weaving, woodworking, or carving enables
them to take the role of specialists. For the most part associational
groupings based on occupational and economic interest, are a phe-
nomenon of modern society and, in part at least, a product of our
increasingly complex division of labor. In an industrial society one's
associations are not primarily with an extended group of kin but
with people who live in the same neighborhood, or who go to the
same church, or who work in the same plant, shop, or office. Ours
is a money economy, and one's status, associates, and satisfactions
are all related to that fact. With most of the rest of the world it is
otherwise.

Every society has methods of producing and distributing goods
and some system of exchange, even though money as such may be
absent. Modern Western societies are distinguished not only in
points of size and degree of complexity, but also by an emphasis on
production for profit and a consequent depersonalization in relationships. This industrial pattern is now spreading to other areas of
the world with resulting disruption of traditional ways of living.
There are, however, still many millions of people whose relation to
the earth is a direct one and who are bound to their relatives and
neighbors in a web of personal relationships and mutual obligations without which they could not well exist.

2. Our Daily Bread

Within certain limits all human beings have the same nutritional
needs, but the way in which these needs are satisfied varies so
greatly from one people to another that we may think of each
society as having a nutritional system of its own.

We live in a land of abundance and it is difficult for us to realize that for a large portion of the world's peoples food is a constant preoccupation, for the reason that hunger is an everpresent threat. The only foods available to many peoples of the world are those that can be grown locally, and rarely except in the modern Western world has a regular, abundant, and varied food supply been available to the masses of the people. Even in our own society baby foods, fresh meats, and year-round availability of fresh fruits and vegetables are relatively recent phenomena, the result of modern processing, speedy transportation, and refrigeration. A large portion of the world still eats what it can get in season, and millions of the world's peoples seek their bread one day at a time with no assurance that it can be found. Man's preoccupation with food is in fact much greater and more continuous than his concern with sex, and in most of the world there is a real sense in which hunger may be said to underlie the family as a social unit. That is, the meeting of the nutritional needs involves a complex of food getting, food preparation, and food consumption that occupies a large portion of the family's time and interest and which has important ramifications in the family structure.

In modern Western society the relation of the family to food getting is an indirect one and it is much easier to see this process at work in the simpler cultures. In such cultures the family is usually the primary food-getting unit and only by belonging to a family can one's nutritional needs be met. Moreover an important aspect of the husband-wife relationship lies in their respective responsibilities for the family food supply, and the giving and receiving of food may provide important clues to the whole pattern of relationships and the corresponding rights and duties involved.

Food can be defined as an objectively edible substance, that is, one that is capable of nourishing the body, but edible substances must be culturally defined as food before they will be eaten. Thus what we eat is in large measure determined by the culture in which we live and to some degree by our economic and status position within the society. We can be reasonably certain that what any group of people regularly use as food could, if it were culturally accepted, be used as food by any other people. This means that many substances which most Westerners reject as food are perfectly capable of nourishing the human body—horses, dogs, cats, rats, mice, snakes, snails, grasshoppers, grubs, caterpillars, and numerous insects fall into this category, as does human flesh. In many parts of Africa and Australia, the native peoples would be severely undernourished if they did not make use of a variety of grubs and insects. And while cannibalism was usually a ceremonial rite there are peoples who in the not-too-distant past regarded human flesh merely as food.

Before we put all these practices down simply as outlandish ways, we should ask how our food patterns look to other people. To the orthodox Muslim our use of pork is revolting, and to the orthodox Hindu, the thought of eating beef is almost as horrifying as the thought of eating human flesh is to us. To many peoples a crisply roasted grasshopper is more palatable than a raw oyster. Some East African peoples find eggs nauseating, and Chinese students newly arrived in this country have sometimes become ill at seeing people drinking milk.

The way in which food is defined by one's culture can be illustrated in other ways. There are numerous instances of persons becoming ill after they discovered that what they had thought was delicious fish was really eel or rattlesnake, or that the very palatable stew was made of horse meat, muskrat, or some other objectively edible but culturally rejected substance. On the other hand, it is currently fashionable for gourmet supply houses in this country to feature chocolate-covered ants, French-fried grasshoppers, preserved bumblebees, rattlesnake meat, and the like. Moreover, acute or prolonged hunger can sometimes override cultural conditioning. During World War II many Americans who were made prisoners discovered that they could eat wormy rice, weevily bread and many other things that they formerly would have rejected. A booklet issued by the War Department contained information designed to aid military personnel in determining the edibility of strange plants and animals. It concluded with the advice, "Watch monkeys. You can eat anything a monkey eats, and you can also eat the monkey."

Almost everywhere people have some staple cereal or other food on which they depend and without which they feel inadequately fed. Corn or maize, which the American settlers took over from the Indians, and which became an important food in South Africa, is still almost unknown as human food in most of Europe. Wheat and rye are the basic grains in a major part of the Western world with oats, millet, and maize playing a lesser role. Throughout much of Asia rice, not bread, is the staff of life. In various other parts of the world yams, sweet potatoes, manioc, taro, sago, breadfruit, bananas, or fish may form the basic element in the diet. It is as difficult for people from these areas to adjust to bread three times a day as it would be for most Westerners to adjust to rice, yams, or fish at every meal.

Food has many derived implications beyond that of satisfying hunger. In almost all societies there are preferred foods used on special occasions. In the majority of societies, including our own, the feast is a recognized social occasion that involves much more than the satisfaction derived from the food itself. In Europe white bread once had a status value growing out of its lack of availability to the poor. Among some groups in America, "setting a good table" has a status value for a woman closely related to the status the man achieves by being "a good provider." There are a number of societies in which status is achieved by the growing of food far beyond the possibility of consumption. The American farm wife who prides herself on canning or freezing three times the quantity of food her family can use should be able to understand the Melanesian whose reputation is gauged by the number of yams he leaves to rot in his yam house.

There are few, if any, societies in which the partaking of food is a purely casual, unregulated affair. The culture not only determines in large measure what and when one eats, but with whom one eats, and indeed the whole ritual surrounding the giving and taking of food. Every society has its own etiquette pertaining to food and people who eat with their fingers or out of a common bowl may observe a very rigid code of manners.

Societies vary greatly in their practices with reference to who eats with whom. There are societies in which food may be served to guests but hosts and guests do not eat together; there are societies in which the chief must eat alone, and in some societies no one must see him eat. Although the family is almost everywhere a food-getting and food-consuming unit, there are many societies in which husbands and wives do not normally eat together. In some societies the wife may cook for her husband and send the food to him at a men's clubhouse or other gathering place. In polygamous families each wife may have her own cooking arrangements. Each wife may prepare food for the husband daily, or the wives may take turns in cooking for the husband while each woman prepares food for herself and her own children.

Food, then, is much more than an objectively edible substance that can be used to sustain life. It must be culturally accepted and defined as food by people before it can be used. Its use is intimately bound up with custom and tradition, and is circumscribed by notions of hospitality and ideas of prestige. To understand the role of food in any society requires more than a knowledge of food chemistry and the physiology of the human organism. It requires also a knowledge of the society as a whole and the social ramifications of the total nutritional system.

3. What Shall We Wear?

If we define clothing as anything applied to or put upon any portion of the body for any purpose, we shall need to include not only dress as we know it but also the dog-tooth necklaces worn by the Melanesian and the clay or paint with which the Australian aborigines and the Andaman Islanders decorate their naked bodies. Actually, whether much or little is worn, clothing may serve the demands of protection, modesty, and comfort; function as symbols of sex, age, occupation, status, or ritual condition; serve decorative purposes, or be used to attract the opposite sex. Most peoples use clothing for more than one of these purposes, and there is no people known to us who do not wear something that will fit under this broad definition of clothing.

Clothing as protection against weather is, in a sense, a portable shelter, and in the coldest parts of the world clothing is as necessary for survival as are houses. The loose, flowing robes of the desert nomad protect from heat and blowing sand. In tropical areas there is little need for clothing as shelter though in some areas rain hats are used and in other areas there may be need for protection from the sun or from thorns and briars.

Most of the peoples of the world use dress also to conceal parts of the body in the interest of modesty. Many Westerners have judged the civilization of a people by the degree to which they have adopted Western-style garments; early missionaries often encouraged their converts to adopt Western dress and required that they cover their bodies when attending church. There is, however, no essential connection between clothing and modesty, since every society has its own conception of modest dress and behavior.

Almost everywhere clothing is used for decorative purposes, either to show off one's wealth or to enhance the good appearance of the wearer. In this category are decorations and ornaments, hair dressing, body painting, and various forms of body mutilation, such as tattooing and scarring. Clothing in this sense is an aesthetic expression and as such will be treated in a later section.

Clothing as a symbol of sex, occupation, status, or ritual condition is also widespread. Almost all over the world clothing is used as a sex symbol, and taboos against persons of one sex wearing the garments appropriate to the other are found in many societies. In our own society, women may wear men's clothing but there is the strongest kind of feeling directed against the man who wears feminine attire. The use of military uniforms is both an old and a widespread custom, and numerous societies prescribe forms of dress or ornamentation for the married and the unmarried, the old, and the young. Priestly and kingly robes are badges of office and status, and special mourning garments are found in simple and sophisticated societies alike.

Man has used a variety of materials for the making of clothing. Skins and furs are dressed and used in various ways. Wool is woven or matted into felt. Feathers and animal hair are sometimes used, though mainly for decorative purposes. Grass fibers are sometimes simply fastened to a belt at one end and allowed to fall as a sort of fringe to make skirts or capes, and grass or other fibers are woven or plaited into mats or squares which can be draped about the body. In some areas where suitable trees are found, such as the paper mulberry tree in Polynesia, cloth is made from the inner bark by pounding it into thin sheets. Cloth is woven almost everywhere from wool, cotton, silk, or flax. Today, of course, man-made fibers are widely used.

Most of the peoples in warmer climates have traditionally gone barefoot, but sandals, slippers, shoes, and boots are made in a wide variety of forms and of various materials. Westerners think of shoes as being made primarily of leather, but fur boots, moccasins made of dressed skins, cloth slippers, straw sandals, wooden shoes, and clogs are the typical footwear in many areas.

The spread of Western clothing to areas in which little or no clothing was worn in the past has sometimes produced disastrous results in terms of health and cleanliness. In many such cases, people took over only one part of the clothing complex, that is, the wearing of garments. They knew nothing of the care of clothing and in many cases lacked the necessary equipment for such care. When they had worn no clothing, their bodies got a cleansing shower in the rain, and the bare skin dried quickly in the sun and air. When they obtained clothing a shower meant wet garments that did not dry so quickly as bare bodies, and pneumonia or other respiratory diseases sometimes resulted. Often they had little or no water for washing clothes, even if they had known how to do it. There were no fresh clothes to change into so people usually simply wore what they had until the garments fell apart.

In the more sophisticated areas of the non-Western world Western clothing has become common, especially in urban centers, though in many parts of the tropics Western men's clothing in particular is unsuited to the climate and to the way of life of the people.

4. Be It Ever So Humble

The house, whether a simple one-room hut or a mansion, serves essentially the same purpose the world over: it is a shelter from rain, sun, or cold; it is a protection from enemies, animal or human; it is a place for storing possessions; it is a place to sleep and a center for family life; and sometimes, though not always, a place to cook and to eat. It may or may not be a place where visitors are received. It may have much or little in the way of furnishings, and its occupants are determined by the culturally-defined family structure.

The house in a sense surrounds its occupants with an artificial climate and this is true whether what we are calling a house consists of a windbreak, a cave, a skin tipi, or the modern weather-conditioned apartment heated in winter and cooled in summer by the same mechanical system. It keeps its occupants at least to some degree warm and dry or it protects them from the heat of the sun. It protects their possessions from the weather and enables food to be cooked or other tasks performed that rain or cold might make impossible outside.

The form of shelter used among most peoples is dependent to some extent on locally available materials, although cultural emphasis, the standard of living, the level of technology and many other factors may enter in. The houses of American Indians furnish a good illustration of the variety of solutions that men have found to the common problem of shelter. Indian houses varied from the simple windbreaks of some South American tribes to the great edifices of Mexico and Peru. The Plains Indians used tipis made of long poles covered with buffalo skins. Woodland tribes used conical or rounded frames covered with birch bark. In the Pacific Northwest, rectangular houses were made of cedar posts with planked roofs and walls. In the Southwest, the Navahos made earthen lodges or hogans; the ancestors of the Pueblos built many-storied adobe dwellings that have been called America's first apartment houses.

Nomadic peoples obviously cannot have permanent shelters in any one location though many nomads have a sort of base to which they return periodically. Some nomads have devised extremely efficient shelters that can be carried easily from place to place and can be quickly erected in the new location. The tipis of the Plains Indians and the felt yurts of the Mongolian herdsmen were clearly adapted to the necessities of their nomadic life.

Men everywhere seem addicted in varying degrees to the accumulation of goods and gear, and even when the furnishings of a house are of the simplest there is almost always the need of storing food or of keeping tools and implements and the personal possessions of members of the household. The more settled Eskimos build special rooms or portions of rooms for storing food and equipment and even many nomadic or seminomadic peoples have underground caches where food or possessions are left.

The house serves an important function in providing privacy for its occupants. In almost every society that we know of the house is the private property—whether they own it or not—of the people who dwell in it, and outsiders may enter only if invited. The rules of hospitality may vary but in each community they are clearly understood. Among some peoples even the stranger must be welcomed and given food and shelter regardless of the hour at which he arrives or the inconvenience caused by his coming. In other societies the house itself may be open only to the family that occupies it. In some Melanesian communities visitors may be entertained on the platform outside, but are not asked to enter. In parts of Africa men entertain their guests in a central place or palaver house. Only women visit in one another's huts or, more often, outside around the cooking fire.

Who occupies the house varies from one society to another. In modern America the ideal is for the husband, wife, and children to occupy a house or apartment to themselves; even unmarried adult children living in the same town as their parents are free to set up their own establishments. Relatives, unless too old, too ill, or too poor to live alone are not expected to move in with their children, much less with more distant kin. Yet scarcely more than a generation ago households frequently included grandparents, maiden aunts, and other relatives, and every family with any pretense to status had a guest room.

Where the extended family is the rule the household will be arranged accordingly. The Iroquois longhouse was occupied by an extended family that included the eldest female, her husband, her unmarried sons, and her daughters with their husbands and children. In such households there were usually separate sleeping apartments for each of the smaller family groups but they lived essentially under one roof and functioned as an economic unit.

In polygamous societies, one or another of several arrangements may be made for housing a man's wives and children. In some Muslim countries the wives and children share a common harem which is apart from the more public rooms of the house. Among African polygamists it is almost always the rule that each wife shall have her own hut and her own granary. A chief or a headman may have the huts of all his wives within a single enclosure.

In many societies there are separate houses for young bachelors and in some societies there are dormitory-like arrangements for young girls. In many simple societies there are clubhouses for men, to which they can go to get away from the women and children. Such houses sometimes serve also as storehouses for sacred objects such as masks, drums, gongs, and other paraphernalia used in religious or ritual activities.

House furnishings vary with the culture and with the economic situation and status of the family. In many societies most of the activities are carried out on the floor, and there is little of what we would call furniture. In many simple societies there were no chairs or tables and the family slept on platforms or on mats on the floor. The traditional Japanese house had neither chairs, couches nor beds. In China and in Western society furniture-making is an ancient art which gave way to machine-made products. Today, the use of tables, chairs, and beds has become widespread even in areas where their use was once unknown.

Even when the house consists only of a single room there may be carefully defined rules regarding its use. It may be customary for men to be seated at the right of the doorway or in the front of the house while the women and children occupy another section. There may be a place of honor where no guest would dream of sitting without specific urging on the part of the host.

In the Western world the interior of the house is furnished not merely for the comfort and convenience of the family, but as a symbol of family status as well. In the United States, the extra bathroom, the television set, the electric dishwasher, the clothes dryer, the refrigerator, and the freezer are symbols of middle-class prosperity. At one point on the social scale the split-level house, the picture window, and the barbecue pit are as important as the antique furniture, the oriental rugs, the library, and the art masterpieces are at another. The house is often the most revealing of the many ways in which a family expresses its collective personality and its system of values.

Of nations, they [The Persians] honor most their nearest neighbors, whom they esteem next to themselves; those who live beyond these they honor in the second degree; and so with the remainder, the farther they are removed, the less the esteem in which they hold them. The reason is, that they look upon themselves as very greatly superior in all respects to the rest of mankind, regarding others as approaching to excellence in proportion as they dwell nearer to them; whence it comes to pass that those who are farthest off must be the most degraded of mankind.

HERODOTUS (C. 447 B.C.)*

3. HOW PEOPLE LIVE TOGETHER

1. We All Have Families

In the Modern Western world, the interdependence of human beings is obscured by our emphasis on individualism and by the impersonal nature of many of the relationships characteristic of an urban, industrial, money economy. Only in times of personal or community disaster do many people become aware of the extent of their dependence on others and that there are necessities which money cannot buy. Yet there is a real sense in which we become human only in association with other people, and persons who attempt to live in complete isolation are usually those who already are to some degree detached from reality.

All societies are based on some kind of institutionalized relations between individuals and groups of individuals. People can live together only if there are more or less clearly defined ways of behaving that are understood and respected by most of the people most of the time. In order for life to be manageable, people must be assigned to various categories for various purposes, and patterns of behavior must be set up to guide the conduct of people in

* *The History of Herodotus,* pp. 52-53, translated by George Rawlinson (New York: The Tudor Publishing Company, 1939).

the various categories toward one another. All societies regulate the behavior of the sexes in some fashion and all societies have ways of behaving they regard as appropriate for people of different ages. In the simpler societies one's life is usually regulated in large measure by the system of rights and duties within the kin group. Even in the more complex Oriental civilizations the roles of the family and kin group have remained important unless there has been a deliberate attempt to destroy the pattern as in Communist China.

While it is theoretically possible for a society to have existed without family units we know of no society in which some form of the family is not an accepted pattern. With very rare and minor exceptions the basic—though by no means the only—unit is that of husband, wife, and children. This is not surprising when we regard the nature of man's needs and the human conditions faced by all societies. The society must have some means of satisfying the sexual needs of its members and there must be some economic cooperation by which the physical needs of the group are met. Children must be born and cared for during their period of helplessness, and they must be enculturated and trained to carry on the life of the group as adults. There are, of course, numerous other requirements of living together but these four, the sexual, the economic, the reproductive, and the educational stand out as primary to group survival. In practically all societies known to us, regardless of the variations in structure and regardless of other agencies that operate, these four functions are in some way tied in with the simple family unit of husband, wife and children.

So normal is this pattern to our own society that we have come to think of it as not only right but natural. If, however, we are to understand other peoples we must recognize that although this simple family form is found practically everywhere there are many other forms and variations that exist along with it. It helps in this understanding if we look again at the basic human needs the family meets, at the way different peoples regard marriage and the family, and at the differing emphases on the various functions of the family that are found in different societies.

In most simple societies marriage is not only taken for granted, but is for all practical purposes essential to survival. Not only is a woman dependent on the cooperation of a man to provide for herself and her children, but the reverse is also generally true. In simple societies the accepted division of labor is often such that to remain a bachelor or a widower for any length of time is almost unknown, and such a person would find it difficult to survive with any degree of comfort or well-being. In many such societies men would not marry merely to meet their sexual needs since they have ample sex freedom outside marriage. Sometimes the only brake on complete sex freedom for young people is the incest taboo that forbids sex relations between persons defined as too close kin to one another, yet they consider marriage normal and desirable. It is the personal satisfactions of marriage together with social and economic necessities that make this institution so fundamental in all simple societies.

Although in our own society the family has an economic and educational function, we think of marriage as primarily the concern of the individuals involved and we tend to place the primary emphasis on the reproductive function of the family and the limitation of sex to the married pair. In many other societies the emphases are reversed. Where the social and economic aspects of the family are emphasized marriage becomes the instrument for establishing a relationship between two families, and in that light such practices as the arranged marriage, plural marriages, and infant betrothal seem less strange to us. The limitation of sex to the married pair is regarded in some societies as a relatively minor matter, and, while children are almost always highly valued, actual physiological parenthood may be a secondary consideration.

The actual structure of the family takes many forms. In a great many societies of the world plural marriages are sanctioned, but almost always in these cases polygamy and monogamy exist side by side, the taking of additional wives often being a prerogative of age and high economic status. There are a few societies in which one woman may take two or more husbands (polyandry), but the more usual practice is for one man to take two or more wives (polygyny).

The specific form of the polygamous household varies from society to society, as does the relative position of the women. In some societies there is a senior wife; the younger women all have the status of wives but are under the direction of the first wife. In other societies only the first wife has the formal status of wife; the additional women are considered concubines. Elsewhere a man may have several wives as well as concubines. A good illustration of this pattern may be found in the Biblical story of Jacob's marriage to the two sisters, Leah and Rachel, who both gave him their handmaidens as concubines. The same story illustrates several other practices found in many societies today such as the marriage of one man to two sisters, which is called sororal polygyny, and the so-called bride price which the young man may pay in cattle, goats, money, or a variety of gifts. In some societies the bride price may also be met in the same way Jacob met it—by working for the girl's father.

The notion is prevalent among Westerners that bride-price is a payment by which a bride is purchased. It is true that there is a monetary consideration and the interested families may haggle over the number of cattle or the other payments to be given. There are, however, many other factors involved and nowhere is the wife considered a mere chattel. She is not in the same category as the slave, and no African husband "owns" his wife in the sense that he "owned" the cattle which he gave for her. The whole concept is exceedingly complex. There is a sense in which the bridal payments are compensation to the girl's family for the loss of one of its members; this seems quite evident in those societies in which the cattle given for the daughter are used to obtain a wife for a son. The cattle are also a strong force in stabilizing the marriage and in giving both families incentive for seeing that the couple stay together and fulfill their duties to one another. A man who has given cattle to the girl's family may, if the wife proves an un-satisfactory mate, demand that her family either see that she mends her ways or that his cattle be returned. It is thus to her family's interest that their daughter behave as a dutiful wife, and they may exert considerable pressure to secure that end. On the other hand, a woman whose husband abuses her may flee to her own people for protection. If the man is clearly at fault he cannot reclaim his cattle. Thus he is under pressure to behave as a husband should lest he lose both cattle and wife.

In societies in which the status of women is changing women leaders may deeply resent polygamy, but there are many places in which it is still considered normal by the women themselves and preferable to other alternatives available to them. A senior wife may insist that her husband take other wives partly because it is the accepted thing to do, partly because it adds to the family's status and prestige, and sometimes for the very practical reason that with no servants and no labor-saving gadgets she wants someone to help her with the work. In some societies in which women live rather isolated lives and do not share in the social life of their husbands, the wife may welcome the companionship of another woman.

Polygamy is widely practiced in simple societies, but there is in general no correlation between the complexity of the social patterns and monogamy. Some sophisticated societies have practiced polygamy and concubinage, yet some of the simplest societies known are strictly monogamous. In this country many Mormons practiced polygamy until relatively recent times, and today divorce and remarriage in America have become so common that we are sometimes said to be practicing serial polygamy.

In many parts of the world physiological paternity is of far less importance than sociological parenthood. A man may not be greatly concerned over who is the actual *genitor* or physical father of the child he claims as his own but he will be tremendously jealous of his rights as *pater,* that is, as the legal or sociological father. We, of course, have patterns that are roughly comparable to this in adoption and step-parenthood. The recent interest in artificial insemination is in keeping with this general idea. In this case, of course, the genitor is the unknown donor of the semen that impregnates the mother while her husband is the pater of the child born to her. There are also a certain number of women in our society who have extramarital affairs and who sometimes bear children whose actual paternity is in question. We generally act as if this kind of behavior were unknown and in any case, unless the question is raised by the husband, the children born to the wife are legally those of the husband and he is assumed to be their physiological as well as their sociological father.

In the traditional pattern of many African societies children were legitimatized by the man's giving cattle or other gifts to the girl's family—the Thonga of South Africa had a saying "cattle beget children" based on this concept. What a man received for his cattle was, among other things, the right to his wife's child-bearing capacity—whatever children the wife bore thereafter belonged to him regardless of who their genitor might be. A marriage might be recognized before the cattle were given but in this case any children born of it belonged to the wife's family unless and until the husband made the proper payment. Early missionaries often forbade the giving or receiving of these payments by Christian converts on the assumption that the girls were being sold into marriage. They soon discovered, however, that all kinds of difficulties and complications arose as a consequence of the people's deep feeling that, no matter who the physical father of the child might be, the "true" father was the man who gave the cattle. If the cattle were not given the "true" father was the man who should have received them, usually the mother's father or her brother.

One of the clearest indications of the primacy of the family as a sociological unit lies in the various forms of fictional parenthood found in many areas. These practices are closely related to the passion for children which is characteristic of many societies. It was rivalry as to who could bear the most children to their common husband that led Leah and Rachel to have their handmaidens bear children, which then were regarded as sons and daughters of the legal wives and not of the slave girls who actually bore them.

Similar patterns of fictional parenthood were once common in China and Africa, and in some other areas of the world. In many of these cases there is probably some relation to what we call ancestor worship but which in reality is a belief in the importance to both the living and the dead of continuity in the family line. Hence barrenness might be grounds for divorce or justification for a man's taking a second wife or a concubine. In some tribes in Africa a man who died before marriage might get children through a spirit marriage which his mother arranged for him with a real wife. The wife was accepted into the mother-in-law's home and was expected to bear children for her spirit husband who would be their pater. The genitor or physical father might be a male relative of the dead man, or in some cases any male of the girl's choosing. The genitor was not considered the husband, and had no claim on the girl or the children born to her. There were in some parts of Africa similar patterns by which a childless woman could take the role of husband and pater by "marrying" a young woman who bore children to carry on the older woman's family line.

In an earlier day in China various forms of adoption were current, and both plural wives and concubinage were resorted to in order to provide children. In one such case a member of a Christian church was accused of polygamy. He admitted that he was married to two women, but he protested that this was not really polygamy. He was the only son of his father and he was also the adopted son of his father's brother, who had no children of his own. Both the father and the father's brother were entitled to grandchildren. To meet these obligations, the young man had married one woman to provide a daughter-in-law and grandchildren for his own parents. In his role as adopted son he had married a second woman to provide a daughter-in-law and grandchildren for his adoptive parents. Neither he nor the rest of his family considered this wrong, or even

polygamy in the usual sense of the word—it was, rather, an obligation to the family as a whole.

The family takes other forms, some of which are supplementary
to the husband-wife-children arrangement, and there are others
which may be thought of as an extension of this small group. In
societies in which the family line is carried on through males—as
we carry on our family names—the husband is normally the head
of the household and the guardian of the children. There are, however, a number of societies in which the family line is carried on
through females, in which case the mother's brother may be the
responsible head of the family. In such families a child may inherit
not from his father but from his mother's brother who is responsible
for his upbringing. Usually husband, wife, and children live in the
same household but the father has a duty to his sister's children
and he shares responsibility for his own children with his wife's
brother. In some cases, a man supports his sister and her family
while he, his wife and children, are supported by his wife's brother.

A striking example of this type of family—sometimes called the
consanguineous as against the conjugal family—was found among
the Trobriand Islanders. Husband, wife, and children shared a
common household and fathers were often extremely fond of their
children, but it was the mother's brother who disciplined the child,
gave him his place in the community, and from whom the boy inherited wealth, magical knowledge, status, and rank. The child, its
mother, and the mother's brother belonged to the same clan, and
they formed a family unit for particular purposes—the father,
mother, and child formed a second kind of family unit for other
purposes. Each woman had certain loyalties and obligations to
both units; and each man had obligations to his wife and children,
and certain other obligations to his sister and her children. Although the Trobrianders insisted there was no physiological relation between a man and his wife's children, the birth of a child
established a social relationship between a man and the child born
to his wife. He lavished affection upon the child, and would perform the most intimate and menial services for it. The child in
turn came to feel a strong bond with the man who supposedly was
related to him only as his mother's husband. The bond was explained on the basis of the father's care of the child.

All these patterns seem to add up to the fact that what we think
of as family sentiments can be established irrespective of physiological relationships. It is not the genetic tie as such but the social

definition of the relationship and the sentiments of dependence and affection growing out of the shared experiences of daily life that bind people together.

2. The Broken Family

In all societies known to us marriage involves, to some degree at least, certain major assumptions. There is almost always a recognition of the mutual obligations of the marrying pair, such obligations usually being extended to include certain of their relatives. In almost all societies arrangements in which the woman does not have the full status of a wife are in a different category from formal marriage that is socially recognized as such. There is almost everywhere the assumption that the marriage is expected to be permanent even though it is well known that many marriages do break up, and more or less formal arrangements for handling an unsatisfactory marriage usually exist. All societies known to us have some socially sanctioned provisions for widows and orphans when a marriage is ended by death.

In much of the Orient, and in many other parts of the world, a widow does not normally manage her own life or return to her own family but remains a part of her husband's family, who have a right to the children. In some cases a widow is expected to live humbly as a dutiful daughter-in-law, with no life of her own and no opportunity to remarry. These patterns are in process of change today, but they still persist in many of the rural or more isolated sections of the Oriental civilizations.

By far the commonest practice among people in simple cultures is for the widow to marry her deceased husband's younger brother or some other suitable relative. This practice, called the levirate, was common among the ancient Hebrews and is familiar to us in the Biblical story of Ruth. The levirate is still practiced in many African societies today. A widow is inherited by her husband's younger brother, in some cases by one of the husband's sons of another marriage, or by some other relative of the husband. Such marriages usually follow a fairly prolonged period of mourning and the husband's family usually makes the decision as to which of the appropriate relatives the widow is to marry. She may or may not be given any choice in the matter. The widow past child-bearing age sometimes may, if she wishes, live in a house provided by a son and be under his protection. In some African societies a widow may be permitted to marry or live with some man outside the family group, but any children born of such a union belong to the deceased husband's family. :

Both the levirate and the practice of polygamy on which it is dependent—since the younger brother or other heir may very likely already have one or more wives—are found in societies in which every woman is expected to have a husband, and the role of wife is the only one open to her after she leaves her father's house. To outlaw polygamous marriages before some socially acceptable role other than marriage is established for unmarried or widowed women is practically to condemn them to lives of prostitution.

In many societies the having of children to carry on the family is of such major importance that when a man dies without heirs various fictional arrangements may be made to remedy the situation. The levirate is more than a means of providing for the widow and her children; it may also be the means of keeping alive the husband's family line. The "raising up of seed" to the deceased, and ghost or spirit marriages arranged in the name of the dead man are primarily means to this end.

In some societies when the wife dies—particularly if she dies before she has borne children—her family may be expected to provide a second daughter or other relative to take her place. This form of the sororate is a variation of sororal polygyny in which a man has the right, or more rarely the obligation, to marry his wife's younger sisters as additional wives while the first wife is still living.

Societies vary in their handling of the unsatisfactory marriage. Divorce may be easy or difficult; it may be a recourse open to either husband or wife, or it may be the prerogative of the husband only. Although in some societies the termination of marriage appears rather casual and remarriage is often taken as a matter of course, there is no society known to us in which such matters are entirely unregulated, even if only by public opinion as to what behavior is appropriate under what circumstances. Usually there is some institutionalized provision for terminating the unsatisfactory marriage and almost always there are regulations of some kind—whether embodied in legal codes or merely in custom—by which the rights of the children are in some degree protected.

3. The Extended Family

In many parts of the world, the socially important unit is not the simple family but the larger group sometimes known as the extended family. The extended family consists of several generations held together through the male line (patrilineal) or through the female line (matrilineal). Such a family may occupy a common residence, which may be a large compound with separate apartments for each of the smaller family units, or it may be simply individual huts grouped together. The newly married pair may reside with the husband's people (patrilocal) or with the wife's people (matrilocal). In some societies the young couple may live for a year or two with one of their families, then settle permanently with the other. The Dobuans of Melanesia practiced alternating residence. They spent every other year in the village of the wife's people, and alternate years in the husband's family village. In some societies the young couple may choose where they will live but rarely are they completely free from some form of supervision or control from one or the other of their families.

The traditional Chinese family system was strongly patrilineal and a household consisted of the parents, their unmarried daughters, the sons and the sons' wives and children. As the girls of the family married, each went to live with her husband's people, and generally maintained only such communication with her own people as her husband's family allowed. If a woman was widowed, she continued to live with her husband's family, who were responsible for her and her children. The eldest male—the father and at his death his younger brother or eldest son—became the head of the establishment. A son remained subject to his father's wishes as long as the father lived, and a woman was obedient to her mother-in-law. A woman achieved some status with the birth of a son, but did not really come into her own until she herself became a mother-in-law and the grandmother of her son's sons. A wealthy Chinese family of the past might house in a single compound as many as a hundred persons including not only the persons just named, but also perhaps the widowed mother of the eldest male or the widows and children of other male members of the family. There might also be concubines and their children, servants and, in earlier days, slaves. Such households functioned as economic, social and, to some extent, religious units.

The Navaho provide us with an example of the matrilineal family. In the old days it was generally matrilocal though the husband, wife, and children formed a basic family unit, usually occupying its own house. The extended family group commonly consisted of an older woman, her husband, their unmarried children, and the married daughters with their husbands and children. There might also be other dependent relatives from the mother's side of the house.

Although the extended family does not take over all the functions of the simple family unit, it usually maintains an overall supervision of its members and there are clearly defined rights and duties involved. All extended family units tend to place authority in the hands of the aged members and inculcate respect for elders. There is a corresponding reduction in the authority of young parents. In many Oriental families even today young men are expected to defer to their parents' wishes and the wife is expected to be obedient to her mother-in-law. An American nurse who attempted to set up a well-baby clinic in pre-Communist China received no response at all to the invitations which she had sent to the mothers of the children. When a Chinese friend explained that it was the husband's mother who would make the decision the invitations were sent again this time to the paternal grandmother of each child. This brought forth most of the infants, many of them accompanied by their mothers. It was, however, not the child's mother but the paternal grandmother who decided whether the child should come and who should accompany it.

The clan, found in various societies, is in many ways an expanded and diffused form of the extended family though the two differ in a number of respects. Theoretically, clan members are the descendants of a common ancestor, the descent being traced through either the male or the female line. In patrilineal clans, where descent is traced through the males, the children automatically belong to the clan of their father; in matrilineal clans they belong to the clan of their mother. The extended family usually includes in its membership those who marry into the group, but such persons generally maintain membership in their own clans. The extended family is usually relatively small, lives in the same locality, and the relationships of its members are known. The clan may be very large, may be scattered over a wide territory, and its more distantly related members may be unable to trace their specific relationships to one another even when they regard themselves as clan brothers and sisters. Clans usually have a clan name or a totem emblem by which they are identified and through which relationship can be established. The clan totem is often some animal species and members of the clan are identified as leopards, lions, crocodiles, eagle-hawks, or kangaroos as the case may be. The extended family usually functions as some sort of economic unit; the clan rarely functions in this way though clan members are generally expected to assist one another.

Most clans serve to regulate marriage and one may be forbidden to marry a member of one's own clan. In many African societies one's first duty on meeting a stranger is to ask his clan name, in order that each person may know how to treat the other. Two Navahos would do the same thing. Clan members are often regarded as brothers and sisters and sex relations between them is considered incest. Under such circumstances care must be taken to maintain a proper relationship of respect and social distance between persons of opposite sex.

4. Counting Kin

To Americans, our customary patterns of classifying our near relatives into uncles, aunts, cousins, nieces, and nephews seem so natural and logical that one is apt to wonder how else it could be done. Few people are aware of the principles underlying our methods of grouping these relatives, and most people are surprised to find that there are not only other ways of doing it, but that our way is the exception rather than the rule.

We group these relatives according to generation, and we distinguish lineal from collateral lines. Our terminology designates the sex of all relatives except cousins. We ignore all other possibilities. All the male relatives in one's parental generation, except father, are classified as uncles. All the females in this category, except mother, are aunts. The children of all these persons, along with their spouses are classified as cousins, regardless of sex. The children of our brothers and sisters with their spouses are classified by sex and generation into nieces and nephews.

There are a number of other equally reasonable ways by which these relatives may be grouped and almost all of these ways are followed by one or another people who regard their way as natural and right. Other peoples take into account certain factors we ignore and ignore factors to which we attach importance. In our classification we ignore age, whether the relatives are on mother's or father's side, and whether they are related to us by birth or marriage. We take no account of the sex of the person claiming the relationship, that is, the sex of the person speaking has nothing to do with the terminology he uses.

By far the most common pattern among other peoples is one that bases the major distinctions not only on sex and generation but also on whether a person is related through the father or through the mother. An extremely common pattern of this sort follows the principle of equivalence of brothers. In this case my father and his brothers are classed together; I call them all father and they all call me son or daughter. The wives of these extra fathers become my mothers, and I am a child to them. The own children of these extra fathers and mothers are then, quite logically, not my cousins, but my brothers and sisters. Often, though not always, the principle is extended to include the equivalence of sisters: my mother's sisters then become my mothers, their husbands are my fathers and their children, too, become my brothers and sisters. Siblings of opposite sex are not equated, that is, one does not equate father with his sister or mother with her brother, hence these persons are not parents to me and their children are not my brothers and sisters. Different societies classify these persons in different ways.

The equating of brother with brother and sister with sister leads to a distinction into two types of the relatives we call cousins, one group being treated as brothers and sisters, the other being treated in a quite different fashion. For convenience, the anthropologist designates as "parallel cousins" the children of siblings of the same sex—that is, the children of two brothers are parallel cousins, and the children of two sisters are parallel cousins. Parallel cousins usually address one another by the same term they use for their own brothers and sisters and behave with them accordingly. The children of siblings of opposite sex—that is, the children of a brother and those of a sister—are referred to as "cross cousins" to one another. Sometimes cross cousins are treated in much the same way that we treat cousins; in some societies they are regarded as suitable marriage partners.

It should be understood that the terms "parallel cousin" and "cross cousin" are simply convenient anthropological designations and are not the terms used by the people in question. The terms apply only in societies which regard the relationship of the children of two brothers or of two sisters as being different from the relationship of the children of a brother and a sister. In the societies which make this distinction people often feel very strongly that the relationships are very different. They therefore have no general term that means what we mean by the word "cousin."

There are some societies in which there are no words that can be translated simply as *brother* or *sister*. There are languages in which there is a word meaning older brother and another word meaning younger brother, but no single word that means just brother. The same pattern may be followed with reference to sisters. Furthermore, there are languages in which you cannot refer to your brothers and sisters without taking into account your own sex. In parts of Africa, Oceania, and among some American Indians there is one word that means "sibling of my own sex" and another that means "sibling of opposite sex." Thus a girl calls her sister by the same term that a boy calls his brother. The second term is used by a girl to address her brother and by a boy to address his sister. In each case the terms are extended to the appropriate "cousins."

There are also societies in which there are no words that can be translated as our *niece* or *nephew* because one takes into account the sex of the speaker rather than the sex of the person spoken to. A man uses a single masculine term for his sister's children, and a woman uses a single feminine term for her brother's children.

If these patterns seem peculiar to us, we should remember that we must designate the sex of the persons referred to when we speak of the siblings of our parents or the children of our siblings. There is no single word in English that can refer to either uncle or aunt, and none that means either niece or nephew. In practice we also have to designate the sex of our brothers and sisters since the term sibling to mean either brother or sister is rarely used in ordinary speech. On the other hand, we cannot designate the sex of a cousin without going out of our way to do it by saying my male or female cousin. Neither can we distinguish father's brothers and sisters from mother's brothers and sisters without adding the terms paternal or maternal. This pattern seems peculiar to people whose word for mother's brother is entirely different from the word used for father's brother.

To one unfamiliar with other kinship patterns the terminology of some societies would seem to make literal the song, "I'm my own Grandpa." To hear an elderly male calling a little girl "grandfather" is startling only if we assume that the term which is translated "grandfather" is limited to the meaning we attach to it. To us the term unless qualified by some other word can only mean the male parent of one of our parents. In another society its meaning may well be "the parent of my parent plus all the other persons I should include in the same category."

In some societies grandparents and grandchildren call one another by the same terms. We use this kind of reciprocal term only for cousins or for siblings of the same sex. The person I call cousin also calls me cousin, but the person I call brother calls me brother only if I am a male. In some societies there is one term which the grandchild uses for all four grandparents and which the grandparents in turn use for any grandchild. In other societies there may be a different term for each grandparent, but each of these terms also refers to the corresponding grandchild. In many societies—as, often, in our own—grandparents are more indulgent of their grandchildren than they were of their own children. In one South African society the term a person uses for grandparent means literally, "one who indulges me" while the term a grandparent uses for a grandchild means "one whom I indulge."

The extended relationship terms used in many societies should not be confused with ceremonial or courtesy titles, as when a priest is called Father, or when we speak of Grandma Moses, or refer to some elderly person in the community as Uncle Jim or Mother Jones. Many of the simpler societies also have such courtesy titles. Sometimes any respected older person may be addressed as father or mother or a spirit as grandfather.

Moreover, the people who use extended kinship terms are not confused as to the biological relationships involved. We use the term uncle for the husband of a father's or mother's sister though if asked we would explain that these men are really uncles-in-law. The child in a simple society also knows who is his "true" father though this may mean the pater rather than the genitor. He can also tell you which of his various mothers is the one who gave him birth. Although all persons called by the same term usually are supposed to be treated in the same way, there are varying degrees of closeness which may affect the relationship. A child normally lives in the household of his true mother and feels close to her though he may feel quite free with the mother's sisters whom he calls mother and who treat him much as they treat their own children. A boy owes respect to all his classificatory fathers though he is likely to be closer to his "true" father. Among the Ontong Javanese a boy called his father's brothers "father," but if asked about it he would designate his own father as the "true" one and the others as "stolen" fathers.

All of these patterns will make more sense if we remember that there is a difference in a set of genealogical relations and a kinship system. All peoples have essentially the same genealogical relations, but what is important in human societies is not genealogical relations as such but the way they are defined by the particular society. The kinship system consists of the real or assumed genealogical relationships recognized by the society and, as we have seen, not only can the actual genealogical relationships be defined in various ways but fictional relationships can be assumed.

5. The Function of the Kin Group

A knowledge of these various kinship patterns and their significance explains a great deal of behavior that is otherwise extremely puzzling to an outsider who is unfamiliar with any kinship system but his own. The kinship categories are useful for grouping people into manageable units and for regulating behavior within and between such units. In actual practice the relationship terms serve to define the rights and duties, the privileges and responsibilities, which persons in the various categories have towards one another. The use of relationship terms in reference and in address serves further to express and thus to affirm and strengthen existing bonds as the society has defined them.

Associational groups are minimized in the simple society and most of life's activities are regulated by the network of kinship. These kinship bonds satisfy a multitude of needs. They serve to regulate marriage and to define the rights and duties, not only of the married pair, but of their respective relatives. They assure to each person various other persons who have obligations to him under specified circumstances. They define the proper roles of different people in such matters as arranging marriages, assisting in childbirth, and the rearing of the young; in assigning responsibility for various economic tasks, in providing for illness, old age, and death, and in the transfer of property.

In the modern industrial society these various needs are often, if not usually, met in other ways. There are government agencies and community or commercial enterprises such as orphanages, schools, hospitals, homes for the aged, insurance companies, undertakers, doctors and nurses, banks, loan companies, employment agencies, and numerous other agencies and institutions to which the individual can turn for assistance. In the simple society the individual's needs are met by the appropriate relatives to whom he in turn has duties and obligations.

One extremely important function of the kinship system is the regulation of behavior between people of the same and of opposite sex. The many social and economic functions of the family and kin groups call for the kind of cooperation which would be threatened by sex rivalry. In almost all societies that we know of such rivalry is either ruled out or rigidly regulated within such cooperating groups. There are regulations regarding who may marry whom and regulations regarding incest. The definitions of incest and hence the regulations vary from one society to another, and since they are primarily social rather than biological—though they are usually rationalized biologically—their major importance lies in the way they regulate behavior and protect the family group from jealousy and dissension by removing sexual competition. The definition of persons as fathers and mothers, sons and daughters, brothers and sisters, automatically places them in the category of individuals in whom one does not have sex interest. They are thus not defined as appropriate sex objects to one another.

In simple societies where people live in one-room houses and where no actual privacy is possible, a sort of psychic distance is maintained between people who should not be sexually intimate with one another. In such societies there may be rigid regulations designed to maintain the proper social distance between persons whose union would be regarded as incestuous, and they may be required to behave with great formality toward one another. They may be forbidden to address one another directly, to use one another's names, to be alone together at any time, and, since many societies regard eating together as an act of familiarity, they may be forbidden to eat together or even in one another's presence. In societies that practice the levirate, a woman may be forbidden to eat with her husband's elder brother, but may associate freely with her husband's younger brother who, in the event of her husband's death, would be expected to marry her. Likewise, in societies in which a man may marry two sisters, he may be required to behave with great formality toward his wife's elder sister, but may behave with great freedom toward the younger sister who is a potential wife to him.

It is sometimes assumed that when people in other cultures become Christians or adopt Western patterns of one kind and another they will automatically cast aside such kinship regulations. It is true, of course, that people who reach a certain level of sophistication may allow such patterns to slip into disuse. However, these patterns serve as extremely important instruments of social control and premature abandonment of them may have seriously disrupting consequences in the society. Moreover, human beings do not so easily abandon their culturally-patterned reactions. A woman may be quite aware of the social rationalization that forbids her to eat in the presence of her husband's elder brother and yet, if she does so, she may feel both guilt and shame. The situation may be all the more painful in that she may feel an added guilt at being unable to free herself from what she now believes to be an outmoded pattern of thinking, feeling, and acting.

It is unfortunate that Westerners should have been so unaware of, or so indifferent to, the kinship patterns of peoples of other cultures. Not only are Europeans and Americans generally ignorant of the relationship terms and the accompanying patterns of behavior found in other societies, but they often regard such patterns as a sort of aberration that may be ignored, if not corrected. Yet there are few things more important to effective administration or just behavior than an understanding of such relationships. Many cruel and needless mistakes have been made by missionaries, teachers, employers, or officials who did not know that a young man was obligated to all his father's brothers who were fathers to him or that a young woman might with perfect propriety talk or joke with her father's sister's sons but would be overcome with shame if asked to so much as speak to the son of her father's brother.

> *All the world's a stage*
> *And all the men and women merely players.*
> *They have their exits and their entrances;*
> *And one man in his time plays many parts.*
>
> SHAKESPEARE*

4. FROM BIRTH TO DEATH

1. The Life Cycle

Within broad limits of individual variation human beings every where go through the same life cycle. Birth, gradual development of the organism, eruption of the teeth, walking, talking, sphincter control, muscular coordination, and so on follow much the same sequence everywhere. The onset of puberty and mating; pregnancy, parturition, lactation, and the menopause in females; aging, senility, and death are realities to human beings in all societies. The way in which particular events are interpreted varies from one society to another but no society that we know of ignores them all. An important factor in the life cycle lies in the individual's role sequence. All societies recognize the helplessness and dependence of the human infant, and all make some distinction between the roles of children and adults. There is great variation, however, in the stress put upon the various roles and in what is expected of people at various levels.

Many societies mark the individual's progression from role to role by changing his name, or by giving him designations that indicate each particular role. The Andaman Islanders gave a girl a "flower name" at her puberty ceremony, and she was addressed by this name until she bore her first child. Among the Chaga of East Africa a new baby was referred to by a term meaning "the incomplete"—literally, a being without teeth, and without a name. After the teeth were cut he was referred to as "the little one who fills the lap." His third stage lasted till about three during which he was considered an

* *As You Like It,* Act II, scene 7.

infant. The fourth stage lasted from four to fifteen. Thereafter the children should be old enough to behave as youths and maidens. The Kalingas of the Philippines recognized ten stages in the growth of the child from birth to maturity: "newborn," "beginning to smile," "he creeps," "he sits alone," "he stands up," "he begins to walk," "he runs around," "he can be sent on errands," "he can be sent to the forest for fuel," and finally "companion," which implied full majority. As a companion the boy could fight, court girls, marry, and set up his own household.

Age-graded cultures provide for a formal shift in roles as the individual matures. In such societies each male belongs to an age-set by reason of his birth at a particular time, and he and his age mates are thus persons of approximately the same age. Each age-set moves through a series of age-grades in each of which different rights and duties are involved not only to one's own age mates but also to the preceding and following age-sets. Each person thus moves through life as a member of an age-set, very much as a college student moves through college and becomes an alumnus as a member of a specific class. In the age-set, however, the movement from grade to grade involves changes in the rights and duties, and the individual moves from one grade to another throughout life. Moreover, when the individual takes on new duties such as becoming a warrior, or loses some privileges as he does when power is handed on to the younger men he does so as a member of a group. He is supported not only by the fact that his age mates are experiencing the same shifts in role but also by the fact that the society as a whole expects, recognizes, and approves the shift.

In our own society, the stages of infancy, early childhood, and school days are generally recognized as periods of dependency. If college is among the normal expectations of the family, the period of dependence may continue through college graduation. Thus, whether the child is expected to become independent after grade school, high school, college, graduate school, or upon marriage varies with economic levels as well as with personal or family patterns.

2. The Child Learns His Culture

In all societies birth is a significant event and the reputed casualness of birth in simple societies is not borne out by the evidence. While there are a few societies in which women bear their children virtually unattended, this is not generally the case. Usually female relatives of either the husband or the wife are in attendance, though sometimes attendants are more or less in the category of the professional midwife. Medicinal herbs and manipulation of the woman's body as well as magical rites may be used to insure safe delivery of the child.

The husband's role in the birth is variously interpreted. He may be expected to play an active role or merely to keep out of the way. In some cases he may not be permitted to see either mother or child until a given period has elapsed and certain ritual precautions taken. A custom, or more properly, a collection of related customs, known as the couvade is found in various parts of the world, notably among some South American Indian tribes. Although the specific patterns vary, the essential characteristic of the couvade seems to be that the father takes a symbolic role in the lying-in. Sometimes he is expected to simulate labor pains, and he may remain in bed while the mother is expected to get up and go about her business. Among other tribes both parents may remain in seclusion and observe various food and other taboos for a designated period.

A pattern known to the ancient Hebrews may be found in a number of societies today. A woman is regarded as ritually unclean following childbirth. She may remain in this state for various periods; in some cases the period may differ with the sex of the child, as it did in Mosaic law. In many societies both mother and child may be regarded as particularly vulnerable to evil spirits or sorcery during the early days of the child's life, and special precautions are taken for their protection.

In most simple societies babies are welcomed though, in the past, among some hunting and gathering societies infanticide was a practical necessity when a second child followed too closely after the first one. Among the North Alaskan Eskimos economic conditions were sometimes such that a child was taken from the mother and "thrown away" before it had been given a name, and thus was not yet considered a member of the society. Among some Australian tribes, a second child born before the older one could walk was a hindrance to the family's search for food and was sent back to the spirit world to await a more convenient time for birth.

In all simple societies women nurse their babies, and a child may be suckled for two or three years, sometimes longer. Weaning is often interpreted as the transition from infancy to childhood. In the simple society weaning usually marks the first major role change in the child's life, in that it breaks the child's dependence on the bodily presence of its mother. It may therefore be a far more traumatic and significant break than in our own society in which children frequently are never nursed at the breast and where the change from milk to other foods is made gradually and early.

All societies face the problem of training the developing individual to think, feel, and act in accordance with the patterns of the particular society of which he is a part. It is this process, called socialization or enculturation, by which the infant, hitherto potentially capable of fitting into any culture, becomes an adult who thinks, feels, and acts as a Hottentot, a Navaho, or a middle-class American.

Practically all societies demand certain types of learned behavior before the individual is considered an adult. At various ages the child must adapt to the society's rule for eating and sleeping; learn to eliminate at approved times and places; learn which substances are edible and culturally defined as food; and which substances are regarded as clean or unclean. He must acquire various bodily controls; learn the society's speech patterns, and the appropriate terms not only for objects and acts but for whole categories of persons; learn to observe the society's rules for good manners and for the appropriate behavior in various times and places; accept and adapt to his sex role and sometimes to the status position of himself and his family; learn at least the beginnings of the adaptive techniques appropriate to his sex in obtaining food, clothing, and shelter; and begin to establish the appropriate sentiments toward the value system of the society.

This rather formidable list could be expanded in endless detail. The content of the learned behavior varies, of course, with the particular society. Children are not socialized or enculturated in a vacuum but within the context of a specific society that has specific patterns, procedures, and values. The child does not learn to be "modest"—rather, the small boy learns to keep his pubic leaf in place, or not to expose himself in the presence of girls and women; the small girl learns to sit with her legs together, or to put on her grass skirt, or to cover her face when a tabooed relative appears. Nor does the child learn to be "polite"—he learns to say thank you for a gift, or to take it in both hands, or to take it with his right hand while the right arm is supported by the left hand. The parent or teacher may admonish the child to behave modestly or to mind his manners, but such admonitions are always perceived in terms of particular ways of behaving in particular instances, and within a given culture.

As the child is born into a particular sociocultural context the routines of the society come to seem natural as well as right to him. He learns many things from the way he is held and handled, and from the daily rhythm of life going on around him. The child in our society who never sees his father help with the dishes or household chores, no matter how rushed or weary the mother may be, is learning something of the sex roles of men and women as his own family defines them. The African child whose family eats a large meal at the end of the day and then has nothing but cold snacks until the next evening meal has a conception of mealtime that is quite different from that of the child in our society, to whom three meals a day come as a matter of course. The youngster who grows up in a society in which all father's brothers are considered fathers accepts this arrangement as both natural and right.

The child is constantly subjected to approval or disapproval expressed in various ways by parents, siblings, other relatives, his peers, his teachers, or other individuals. He learns by trial and error, by precept and example, by the language categories used, by imitation of parents and older siblings, and from his peer group activities. He encounters smiles and frowns, facial expressions of pleasure or disgust, withdrawal, caresses, shame, ridicule, praise, blame, physical punishments, deprivations, threats, promises, and incentives. He is admonished and warned of the consequences of his behavior and the possibility of supernatural as well as social sanctions. He is told myths, stories, and legends. He may be encouraged to imitate grown-up tasks in his play. He may learn as an apprentice to his elders or he may be encouraged to experiment on his own. Of very great importance to him are the rites and ceremonies of the society which he may witness and which, in some cases, he may be permitted to share.

In all cultures the child must learn who he is, who other people are, and to play his proper role as the culture defines it in his relationship to objects, to other people who make up his real world, and to the spirits, ancestors, or gods who are also a part of his total experience. Basic to all other learned behavior is that of becoming a full member of his own sex and fully related to the opposite sex. Children in all societies learn their sex roles, in part at least, through their association with their parents or parent surrogates, with whom they identify as of their own or the opposite sex. Children also learn their sex roles in part through play in which they mimic their elders. Plains Indian girls in their play pitched and broke camp, cooked food, and transported their tents on the march. Their brothers hunted rabbits, shot at targets, or set up military clubs. Among the cattle-keeping tribes of Africa, children built play huts of sticks and leaves. The little girls played at cooking porridge; while the boys filled play kraals with their "herds" and with their spears undertook to protect their households.

In practically all societies the child's parents play a large role in the process of enculturation, but in most non-Western societies the extended family or other relatives also play an important part in the child's training. In many African societies children spend many of their early years with their grandparents where they are taught not only skills but tribal lore and values. Among some peoples it is the mother's brother rather than the actual father who has the voice of authority as far as the upbringing of the child is concerned.

In any society the socialization process may be said to be successful to the extent that the values of the society become internalized in the form of sentiments, and the individual develops an inner monitor or "conscience." He is then able to think, feel, and act as the society requires with a minimum of external controls. Where a culture is stable and relatively simple, the cultural expectation tends to be clear-cut and predictable. In modern urban society the problem is more difficult, for the child is exposed to a confused image and contradictory expectations.

3. Achieving Adulthood

All societies recognize the difference in youth and adulthood but they define adulthood in different ways and they vary in the processes by which the transition is made. Some societies look on the transition as one simple bridge quickly and easily crossed; others see it as a series of steps lasting over a long period. Adulthood may come by way of initiation, with economic independence, or upon marriage. Full adulthood may be achieved only with parenthood, and in some societies one takes on the full adult role only upon the death or incapacity of one's own parent. In our own society we achieve adulthood gradually, and we define it differently for different purposes. We have such legal concepts as the "age of consent" for females, and the age at which males or females may contract a legal marriage without parental consent. There are voting ages, ages at which one may hold office, and at which one may sign a legal contract. There are laws regulating the age at which one may leave school or take certain jobs.

Many societies mark the transition from childhood to adulthood by puberty ceremonies for youth. In a large number of societies a girl's first menstruation is occasion for more or less elaborate ceremonies and the event is a matter of public interest and family rejoicing in her new status. In some societies the girl may be secluded for a time. She is sometimes put under the care of female relatives or of older women who teach her how she should treat her husband, her duties toward her mother-in-law and other relatives of her husband, and whatever else the particular society thinks a young woman should know. She may go through various ritual treatments of her body to mark her new status. In some societies her skin will be tattooed or scarified, her teeth may be filed or blackened, or her ears or nose pierced to receive ornaments. In some societies girls are ritually deflowered, and in others the girl may undergo clitoridectomy or other genital mutilation considered necessary as a preparation for marriage. In a number of societies the girl acquires a new name with her new status.

Puberty ceremonies for boys are usually group affairs though in some American Indian tribes the young man went out alone to seek his vision. In many parts of Africa and Australia the initiation ceremonies involved weeks or even months in a bush school or initiation lodge some distance from the village. The training frequently involved physical hardening, tests of skill and endurance, rigid discipline, and education in tribal lore. Many such ceremonies involved scarification and other forms of bodily mutilation.

The puberty rites almost always take the form of what are called *rites de passage,* which mark the passage of the individual or group from one status to another. In such rites the individuals involved are usually taken outside the community both physically and psychologically, in that as far as possible they are cut off from their former way of life. They may be kept awake long hours, required to eat strange foods, and to endure various unaccustomed hardships. At the end of the period the initiates, often dressed in new clothes and given new names, are returned to the community with great fanfare in their new status as adults. The initiation ceremonies have been referred to as a psychological weaning or a ritual cutting of the apron strings. Girls' puberty rites perform something of the function of the debut in our society. They inform the public that a young woman has left childhood behind and has achieved marriageable status.

In some societies young people are permitted to go through a period of sexual experimentation as a prelude to adulthood and marital responsibilities. A number of societies in various parts of the world have bachelor houses in which the young men live and in some of which young men and young women stay together. Other societies have similar dormitory-like arrangements for girls. These arrangements are never completely unregulated affairs, and in a number of societies which seemingly allow a large amount of sex freedom there is a strong condemnation of premarital pregnancy.

In contrast to the sex freedom allowed in some societies, other peoples place great emphasis on premarital chastity of girls. In the old days among the Zulu of Africa a special cow was given to the mother of a virgin bride to honor her for having carefully guarded her daughter. The bridal payment was reduced if the girl was found not to be a virgin, and in some cases the marriage might be called off. The Nyakyusa of Africa had an unusual system of age-villages. It was considered highly improper for a boy to live in the same village with his mother or the other wives of his father and for a girl to be in the same village with her father-in-law. Boys of the same age established villages of their own in which they built sleeping huts, though they still returned to their parental homes for food. Later, when the boys were old enough to marry, they took their wives to the village which then became their permanent home. As boys built the sleeping huts at an early age and as the girls married young this arrangement took all young people out of the parental village before they were old enough for any impropriety to develop. The Nyakyusa believed that sex instruction should come from one's peers or from slightly older youth. It was considered highly improper for parents or other adults to discuss such things with their own or other people's children.

In almost all non-Western societies marriage traditionally has marked the point at which a girl passes from under the protection and power of her own family to that of her husband and his family. Even in societies having matrilineal extended families or clans the girl's marriage symbolizes a change of status with reference to her own family and the transfer of certain rights and obligations from the girl's father or brother to her husband.

In the great majority of the societies of the world marriages are arranged between family or kin groups on the basis of a number of social factors in which the mutual attraction of the marrying pair may play only a minor role. There are a number of societies, very stable ones, in which the betrothed couples do not see one another until their wedding day, and in some cases children may be betrothed as infants or promises made between families regarding children as yet unborn. Even when there is some freedom on the part of the marrying pair, family considerations may be the major factor in the final choice. To people in such societies our practice of "marrying for love" appears to be no more than basing the marriage choice on sexual attraction or mutual infatuation. They find it shockingly immature to arrange a supposedly lifetime partnership on such a flimsy foundation. It does not follow that arranged marriages are marriages without love though, of course, this may sometimes be the case. In general, however, such people feel that in a marriage in which care is taken to see that the match is suitable love will normally follow. The arranged marriage serves the purpose of making sure that each woman is provided with a husband. She is not, as in our culture, left with the responsibility of handling so important a matter alone with the consequent uncertainty of finding a mate at all, much less a suitable one.

The actual marriage ceremony itself is likely to carry a rather heavy load of ritual practices designed to symbolize and express the significance of the event to the individuals, their families, and the community. Our own practices have a large share of such rituals. The engagement and wedding rings, the white dress and veil of the bride symbolic of her virginity, the separation of the bride's family and friends from those of the groom in the seating arrangement at the church, the giving away of the bride by her father, the throwing of rice, the bridesmaids and groomsmen, the display of wedding gifts, the horseplay of tin cans and old shoes tied to the groom's car, the honeymoon, the carrying of the bride over the threshold of her new home—almost all of these patterns can be matched with similar ones in any number of societies throughout the world.

In many societies the marriage is marked by an elaborate exchange of gifts and feasts that may extend over a long period. In a number of societies the groom's family should supply the bride's wedding garments. In other societies the bride should bring to the marriage not only her own trousseau but her own mats or linens or household goods in much the same way as the American bride of an earlier day spun and wove the linens for her future household.

In the majority of societies in the world each individual normally makes his greatest break in role behavior in the shift from his place as a son or daughter in the family in which he grew up—his family of orientation—to his place as husband or wife and parent in his family of procreation. To be sure, he may, for a considerable portion of his life, play both roles as when he still acts as the child of his own parents in his relations with them while fulfilling the role of parent and head of the household to his own children. Moreover, as his parents grow old he may find a shift in his role with reference to them, particularly if they become economically dependent or ill and helpless in their later years.

4. When People Grow Old

Generally speaking, old people in the great majority of societies of the world are respected and deferred to as long as they retain their faculties. In the nonliterate society there is a particular reason for the high status of the elders—they are the repositories of tribal lore and wisdom. In the absence of written records the accumulated experience of the years gives to older people a role of authority. They are likely to be of particular help when experience with the supernatural is needed and such qualifications may more than offset the handicap of failing physical powers. There seems to be a strong correlation between the great honor and reverence shown to the aged and the special relation between the living and the dead, generally referred to as ancestor worship. In societies in which the dead are presumed to influence the lives and fortunes of the living, the old ones are on their way to becoming ancestral spirits, and as such become an important link between the living and the dead.

In most of the societies of the world people take pride in their advancing years which bring increasing power and prestige. In many Oriental and Latin American societies birthdays are occasions of great fiestas, and the "big birthday" marking the end of each decade is of special importance. No one would think of concealing his age, and to be called "grandfather" or "the old one" is a mark of respect. The American cult of youth, in which both men and women are under tremendous social and economic pressure to look and act as young as possible, is wholly incomprehensible to most of the peoples of the world.

Many societies have ways of recognizing and rewarding the advancing years and achievements of their members. Since in most societies the bearing of children is woman's primary role, she may be honored in proportion to the number of children she bears. Among the Chaga of Africa a woman's progress through life was marked by recognition of her maternal role and the increasing respect expressed in honorary titles. When she had borne her first child she was addressed by the name of her paternal great-grandfather in recognition of the fact that she would continue the family line. When she had borne three or four children people said of her, "May she live long, the mother of children." If still more children were born and her eldest son proved his worth she was addressed as "one who had not nursed children in vain." When her sons married she was honored by the title, "the uniter of men" and when her daughters were chosen for wives she was called "the uniter of women." When she became the guardian and tutor of her grandchildren she was greeted as "the exhausted one," a title which indicated that she had been depleted by her children and grandchildren.

Advancing age among men often carries additional honor or prestige, until they reach the point of physical incapacity or senility. In some East African societies men passed from the grade of warriors to that of elders with specific duties and responsibilities. Among some South African tribes all men who had reached mature age had the right to wear a wax ring on their heads as a mark of their status. At a given time the chief informed the eligible men that it was time to prepare their rings. A circular frame was formed and fastened into the hair, then covered over with jet black wax. The ring was not only a symbol of mature age but assured its wearer of certain privileges. Men who wore rings no longer were expected to carry burdens on their heads—each man was assigned a boy to carry loads for him.

In societies in which a premium is put on physical stamina or in which moving about is necessary to survival, the old ones may become a burden when they are no longer physically fit. However, even in the few societies in which old people were abandoned or put to death, there was generally no lack of honor or respect and the killing was either rationalized or was an actual necessity for survival. Some peoples believed that in the future world one continued to live in the same state in which one left this world—thus, to linger on until one was feeble would be to spend eternity in such a state.

There are some societies, our own among them, in which the elders may be paid scant respect, and there are always individuals who fail in their filial duty to their aged and infirm parents. In most of the world, however, those who live to be grandparents seem to find their status a rewarding one that makes up in prestige and power what it lacks in physical health and vigor.

5. When People Die

All human groups must come to terms with the fact of death. They must do something about the body of the one who has died and they must do something about the family disrupted by the death. When the deceased is a child or a youth, only the immediate family may be concerned, but when death takes husband, wife, parent, or some important member of the group the whole community becomes involved. Everywhere people accept the fact of grief and almost everywhere there are patterns of mourning. And always people must face the ultimate mystery of death—what and where is the life that has departed from the body?

There are a limited number of ways of disposing of the physical remains of the dead. The most common disposal is that of ground burial though there are a number of peoples who place the body on a platform in a tree or elsewhere. A sophisticated method widely used in India and in scattered places elsewhere is cremation of the body. Perhaps the most unusual method is that of the Parsees who, unwilling to contaminate earth, fire, or water with the body, expose the dead to be eaten by vultures.

In some societies the body is disposed of almost immediately; in other societies it may be buried temporarily or allowed to decompose, after which the bones are retrieved. The Andaman Islanders either buried the body or placed it on a platform in a tree. At the end of the mourning period they retrieved the bones. The skull and jawbones were decorated and attached to a cord to be worn around the neck on ceremonial occasions. Other bones might be kept in the roof of the hut and the small bones were strung together and given away as presents to be worn to prevent or cure illness.

The possessions of the deceased may be inherited by his relatives but in many societies it is believed that they should be buried with him or destroyed. In a number of societies the hut in which a person dies is either abandoned or destroyed. In other societies it may be purified by ritual means. The pattern of burying some of the dead person's possessions with him is very old and very widespread and is assumed to be recognition of his needs in the next world. Sometimes the weapons or pots are broken and garments or mats may be cut in order that they, too, may "draw the last breath."

In many societies the touching or handling of a corpse is thought to produce ritual contamination, and persons responsible for the burial may be required to undergo some form of purification before they are permitted to resume normal activities. This idea, too, is both old and widespread. It will be remembered that according to Mosaic law touching a dead body rendered one unclean.

Various taboos may be observed during the interval between death and burial or even during the entire mourning period. There are wide variations in such practices even in the same general area. In some African societies a death might be followed by almost complete sex license but among others, sex relations might be forbidden altogether.

Almost all societies have some culturally channeled expression of grief and some period of mourning for the dead. Usually the more important the individual the greater the ritual surrounding his death. In many societies the widow or widows of an important man may be expected to shave their heads or even gash their bodies. They may be expected to leave their hair uncombed and their bodies unwashed. They may tear their garments, paint the body, or smear it with ashes or clay. They may be required to wail or they may be expected to go into seclusion.

When mourning is ended, a reintegration of the mourners into the group takes place. Death is disruptive, and for those whose lives are most affected the mourning period constitutes an important *rite de passage* by which the individuals concerned change their status and at the end of the period reorient themselves to the community.

All societies are confronted with the fact that the person they have known is no longer present and there is an almost universal belief in the continued existence of the person at least for a time in the form of a ghost or a spirit. People may believe in a shadowy world where people go after death; they may believe that people are rewarded or punished in a heaven or hell; they may believe in a continuous wheel of reincarnation, or an ultimate absorption into some kind of cosmic spirit. In many simple cultures the spirits of the dead may be thought to be malevolent beings who seek to wreak vengeance on those who have mistreated them, or they may be regarded as waiting about to be reborn in some of their descendants.

We do not think of the dead as still being members of the community, but there are many societies in which death marks only a change in social personality and social status. In many African societies the ancestral spirits remain as functioning members of the family, lineage, or clan. They are in a position to exercise authority over their descendants and they must be treated with honor and respect. The relation between the dead and the living is really a continuation of their former relationships. The living honor the ancestors by sacrifices and offerings and by behaving in ways the ancestors would approve. The ancestors, in turn, reward or punish their descendants according to their deserts. The ancestor who has not had a sacrifice offered in his name or who has been neglected in other ways may cause illness or may fail to come to the aid of his descendants when they are in trouble or need.

In many simple societies people believe that except for the very old or the very young death does not come from natural causes. Therefore, when a death occurs the question may be, not what, but who, is responsible. In many cases witchcraft, sorcery, or evil spirits are explanations. This does not mean that people may not know that a man was struck by lightning or attacked by a crocodile. The question still remains as to who directed the lightning to the particular spot where the man was, or who caused the crocodile to be in that particular place at that particular time.

One comforting belief held by many peoples is that when an infant dies the soul may enter the mother again and be born a second time. Among some American Indians it was believed that the dead child's spirit stayed in the roof of the hut until it again entered the mother's body. Among some Australian tribes the spirit was believed to return to the totem center to be born again at a later time.

I think a poor life is lived by anyone who doesn't regularly take time out to stand and gaze, or sit and listen, or touch, or smell, or brood, without any further end in mind, simply for the satisfaction gotten from that which is gazed at, listened to, touched, smelled, or brooded upon.

CLEMENT GREENBERG*

5. THE EMBROIDERY OF LIFE

1. The Search for Beauty

We are apt to think of aesthetic appreciation as something limited to people of leisure and a degree of sophistication. People in the simpler cultures may not have too much time for nonutilitarian pursuits, and the peoples who must depend on hunting and gathering their food cannot be burdened with many things to carry around. Yet from the earliest times known to us men seem to have felt that beauty is its own excuse for being and the search for beauty is a universal human experience.

The stone and bone tools of early man often showed more care in form and design than strict utility would require and the paintings left on the walls of European caves show, even in this early period, a remarkable artistic skill. In every part of the world today we find evidence of man's continuing interest in creative expression and aesthetic appreciation. There is no group known to us which does not have some characteristic form of art. The Australian aborigines had an extremely primitive technology, yet they decorated their spears and shields and made elaborate sand or earth paintings. Andamanese pygmies, who have one of the simplest cultures known, painted their bows and arrows and decorated their baby slings with shells. For people with more leisure and more stable abodes various art forms may become highly elaborated and stylized, and all sorts of

* Clement Greenberg. "The Case for Abstract Art," in *Adventures of the Mind*, edited by Richard Threslsen and John Kobler (New York: Alfred A. Knopf, Inc., 1960), p. 253. Copyright © 1959 The Curtis Publishing Company.

63

objects have furnished outlets for man's creative impulses and his aesthetic interest.

Different societies have chosen different media in which to express themselves, and a people may have highly developed art forms in one medium and be wholly indifferent to the possibilities offered by other media that are equally available to them. We are apt to think of painting and sculpture as the major channels of expression in the graphic and plastic arts, but many peoples of the world have depended primarily on other forms. The Maya, Aztec, and Inca Indians developed architecture, weaving, carving, pottery, and metal work. The California Indians, on the other hand, centered their attention on basketry, in which they developed unusual beauty of form, texture, and decoration.

In trying to talk about the art of other peoples we encounter the same difficulty that we find in discussing religion or language or any other aspect of culture. It is difficult not to put ourselves into one category; everybody else, regardless of the differences among them, become "the others" as if not being like us made them all alike. Even if we exclude the Oriental civilizations and limit ourselves to the art of tribal peoples the difficulty remains, for there are striking differences in the art of the various cultures that we thus group together. To use the term "primitive art" as descriptive of the aesthetic expressions of these cultures is even more misleading. All existing art styles are the product of long experience and development, and each culture has developed its own configuration of associated ideas. The artist in any culture operates within certain accepted conventions. The emotions with which persons respond to art are stimulated not by the form alone but by the meaning it has to people who share a system of ideas and symbolic behavior.

It should not be too difficult for us to accept the fact that appreciation of different forms of art, whether of painting, sculpture, music, dance, drama, or literary form, is a learned response. It is commonplace that many now fully appreciated musical compositions were rejected when first performed, and we know that modern music and art meet varying responses in our own culture today. Our concern here is not a comparison of the relative merits of the aesthetic expressions of different peoples. Rather it is that all peoples do have such expressions that to them are meaningful and satisfying. There can be no arbitrary standards that apply everywhere for one's response to any aesthetic expression is in large measure a function of his own cultural experience.

It is sometimes assumed that only in the more sophisticated societies do people come to appreciate art for art's sake, or create art forms simply for the aesthetic pleasure they give. It is true, of course, that objects of art designed solely for aesthetic satisfaction are more commonly found in sophisticated than in simple societies. It does not follow that the peoples of the simpler cultures may not be interested in art for art's sake. The difference is not so much that in the simple society artistic skill is used mainly on utilitarian or ceremonial objects, but rather that there is no clear-cut dichotomy between the utilitarian and the aesthetic. Just as religion in the simple society generally permeates all of life and is not set apart in something called a church, so the aesthetic impulse may find expression in any aspect of life. When the artist uses the walls or posts of his house, the prow of his canoe, the handle of his knife, or the surface of his shield as a field for his aesthetic expression he may simply be using whatever object or surface is available and suited to his artistic purpose. The fact that the decoration does not add to the utility of the object seems to put his work into the art for art's sake category.

Neither is the use of art as a medium of religious expression limited to the simpler cultures. Some of the early Hebrew stories carry detailed accounts of the artistic embellishments of their ceremonial objects, including temples, altars, and the robes of the persons who performed priestly functions. Hindu temples are filled with carvings and paintings, and Buddhist temples and statues are found throughout South and Southeast Asia. The great art galleries of the Western world hold evidence of the long period when the artists of Europe were occupied with the decoration of churches and the portrayal of religious subjects.

While many of the aesthetic activities of the simpler societies are carried on by any person who has the skill required, there are in many areas specialized groups of artists and craftsmen. In the heyday of the great kingdoms of West Africa the economic and social organization was so highly developed that it was possible for the ruling class to support professional artists. The exquisite weaving, pottery, and metal work among the Andean Indians at the time of the conquest was clearly the work of professionals. In some parts of Melanesia grotesque ceremonial figures were carved by professionals, who were paid well for their masterpieces by the rich patrons who had commissioned them. These pieces were sometimes shown in special exhibitions.

There are other simple societies today in which there are professional artists in the sense of highly trained specialists who are rewarded in one way or another for their work. There are in Southeast Asia and some parts of Oceania highly skilled dancers, and some African groups have professional musicians. The Navaho place high value on skill in the ceremonial arts such as dry painting, singing, dancing, and story-telling. Kluckhohn and Leighton suggest that a Navaho singer who knows a single nine-night chant must learn at least as much as a man who sets out to memorize the whole of a Wagnerian opera including the orchestral score, every vocal part, all details of the setting, stage business, and each requirement of costume.

We do not know why a people may produce a high level of music, painting, or drama at one period and be relatively sterile or decadent at another time. It does seem fairly clear, however, that we must look to individual and cultural factors, and not to racial differences as an explanation. Almost all civilized countries have shown such periods of flowering and decline. China, Greece, Italy, Germany, France, and England have had periods of greatness in art, music, or literature followed by relatively sterile periods which produced no outstanding contribution in these fields.

In his *Primitive Art,* Boas points out that in the narrow field of art that is characteristic of each people the enjoyment of beauty is quite the same as among ourselves—intense among a few, slight among the mass. What distinguishes modern aesthetic feeling from that of the peoples of the simpler cultures is the manifold character of its manifestation, which is in turn related to the complexity of the culture. It is, Boas concludes, the quality of their experience, not a difference in mental make-up, that determines the difference between simple and sophisticated societies in art production and art appreciation.

We see that man everywhere has added a plus quality to the utilitarian necessities of living. Everywhere we find some kind of aesthetic expression and appreciation—graphic and plastic arts, oral or written literature, music, song, dance, and drama. Everywhere there are games and a variety of other activities in which people engage just for the fun of it. The specifics and the details vary enormously, but the common core remains. The basic explanation for the universality of this common core seems to be in man's capacity for aesthetic enjoyment and satisfaction that is simply a part of being human.

There is, however, a social function served. Societies vary in the degree to which they foster, encourage, or even allow the aesthetic impulse to find expression, and the forms it takes will vary with the cultural emphasis or expectation. Nevertheless it would seem that some degree of freedom to embroider life is a condition of cultural survival, and that some provision for the relaxation and pleasure of the individual is a social necessity.

There is a sense in which every society punishes its members; it can even be said that such punishment is built into the culture. Everywhere the culture binds and thwarts some of man's natural impulses. People could not live together if everyone did as he pleased without regard for other people, and no society can exist without rules and regulations that act as restraints on natural impulses and personal desires. If people are to be thus restrained there must be rewards to counterbalance the punishments, and satisfactions to match the prohibitions and restraints. Such rewards are something more than the cynical provision of bread and circuses to keep the multitude content with their lot. Aesthetic expression and enjoyment are in themselves rewarding experiences that compensate for much of the dull routine and humdrum activities of daily life. Dress, ornamentation, and body decoration enhance the individual's feeling of self-esteem. Games and recreation provide release from tension and make people both more willing and more fit to take up again the trivial round and common task. The dance, the drama, and the ceremony take one out of the commonplace into areas where the imagination is stimulated and the emotions heightened.

Moreover, in shared experiences the individual loses himself in the group activity. In the prescribed movements of the dance, in the rules of the game, in the words and rhythm of the chant or song, the individual not only subordinates himself to the pattern of the whole but does so in a heightened emotional experience that is both pleasurable and satisfying. Thus in the end these supposedly useless and nonutilitarian activities prove to be the most useful and practical of all. They furnish bonds that bind the members of the society together and they act as a powerful cohesive force without which the society could not endure.

2. The Work of Our Hands

Considered from the point of view of the technical problems involved, man has had various types of material to work with. He has had solid materials such as stone, wood, bone, shell, and ivory; skins and flexible fiber such as sinews, the wool and hair of animals, silk, and vegetable fibers. There are a limited number of ways in which a given material can be handled but there is an infinite variety in the uses to which materials can be put and in the designs and artistic embellishments that can be employed.

Among most of the simpler cultures today stone work is not of major importance. It was, however, one of the materials widely used by early man in the making of tools. Its use in other forms is exhibited in the monumental stone figures of Easter Island and particularly in the architecture and sculpture of the Middle American and Peruvian Indians. The abandoned cities of the Maya in Yucatan and Guatemala show many-chambered palaces and temples, and many of their buildings were elaborately decorated inside and out with relief sculpture. There were stone staircases, gateways, ball courts, baths, vaulted bridges, and carved stone monoliths. The Inca employed professional architects, and were able to cut and fit stone with almost incredible precision.

Ivory, bone, and shell are used as ornaments but also as a field for carving. Carved tusks and figures of various kinds were made in Benin and other West African countries. Eskimos have long used ivory, antler, and bone to make representational carvings and etchings. Many of their small implements are carved in small animal figures just for the pleasure of creation.

Wood carving is widespread and takes many forms. Almost everywhere that wood is found it is used for artistic as well as practical purposes. It is carved, painted, or polished to decorate utilitarian objects; it is made into objects for ceremonial use; and it is carved simply for aesthetic expression. One of the most striking and widespread uses of wood carving is in the ceremonial masks that are found almost all over the world. Sometimes lifelike, but more often grotesque, and often painted and embellished with other materials, these masks are found throughout the Americas, in equatorial Africa, and in Oceania. They were at one time an important element in the primitive cults of Korea.

Among many peoples the skilled potter developed his craft far beyond its utilitarian function and became more artist than craftsman. Not only different groups but individual potters have developed their own designs and there is a wide variety in shape, design, decoration, and the selection of colors. In an earlier period Peruvian pottery was particularly striking in concept and execution.

Jars, bowls, urns, and flasks were made in human and animal effigies.

The use of metals came relatively late in human history and many of the more isolated peoples never developed an extensive metallurgy. In the New World iron smelting was unknown to the Indians and metal tools of any kind were rare. Yet metal working as an art was highly developed among a number of Indian peoples. The Andean metal workers were particularly skilled in work with copper, silver, and gold. The Aztec goldsmiths had a guild, and their gold and silver articles were sometimes decorated with turquoise inlays or set with precious or semiprecious stones. Iron working was widely practiced in Africa from an early period, and ornamental metal work was highly developed in brass, bronze, gold, and silver. The Benin workers used bronze to make cups, bells, stools, staffs, masks, statuettes of human figures, and massive doors. The Ashanti were known for their work in gold and silver, and were noted for the tiny brass figures in various shapes and designs used in weighing gold dust.

The most important of the textile arts are basketry, matting, plaiting, and the weaving of spun fibers. Baskets are made almost everywhere that suitable materials are found, and they have been put to almost every conceivable use. American Indians make burden baskets, water bottles, shallow bowls and trays, cradles, knapsacks, satchels, boxes, and even cooking utensils of basketry.

We think of France, Italy, and the Orient as masters of the textile arts, but some Africans and American Indians with only crude hand looms created textiles of extraordinary beauty. The Peruvians used both cotton and wool to create textiles that compared favorably with the best work of the Chinese or the sixteenth-century Europeans. They used variegated colors and designs in their tapestry weaving and are said to have invented more different techniques of weaving than any other people on earth. West Africans, too, developed weaving into an art.

Other arts occasionally found include beadwork, embroidery, and featherwork. A number of American Indians used beadwork after European traders introduced beads. Plains Indians used colored porcupine quills for embroidery before beads were brought in. In the Cameroons in Africa beadwork was highly developed and gourds covered with beads were used by chiefs on ceremonial occasions. Featherwork was a striking development among some Polynesian peoples and among the Central American and Peruvian Indians.

An unusual aesthetic expression is that of the Navaho dry painting usually called sand painting. The field for the painting may
be a buckskin spread on the ground or a layer of clean, light-colored
sand. The designs are formed of charcoal and minerals or vegetable
materials such as pollen, meal, and crushed flowers. The dry painting designs represent the stories of the Holy People or abstractions
of sacred powers. The paintings are highly stylized and are often
strikingly beautiful. They have been compared to the medieval glass
paintings to make visible and concrete the holy figures and religious
concepts of the people. The paintings are a part of a complex
religious ceremonial and are destroyed when the ceremony is com-
pleted.

Many of the objects made by man are designed primarily for
utilitarian or ritual use. This brief overview makes clear, however,
that nowhere have men been satisfied with the strictly utilitarian.
Man has used the resources of his habitat to make the things needful for his comfort and welfare, but he has also chosen to make the
needful beautiful, and at times he has created objects solely for
the aesthetic pleasure of the maker or of those who can appreciate
his handiwork.

3. The Decoration of the Body

An almost universal form of aesthetic expression is that of body
decoration. This may take the form of clothing, the wearing of
ornaments, dressing the hair, the use of cosmetics or other agents to
dress or color the skin, and various forms of body mutilation. As
we have already noted, clothing may serve various purposes but regardless of the other factors involved, it is almost always a means of
aesthetic expression as well.

The use of ornaments and jewelry as body decoration is known
from ancient times and is almost universal today. Ornaments may
be attached to clothing or to almost any part of the body itself and
almost any object from precious stones to feathers, seeds, fresh or
artificial flowers, human hair, and even human jaws and teeth may
be fashioned into decorative objects to adorn the person.

Hair dressing is one of the commonest modes of altering the
appearance of both men and women. Men as well as women may
shave their heads, wear wigs, or dress the hair in braids, queues, or
topknots. The ancient Egyptians shaved their heads and wore wigs;

the Arunta of Australia pulled hair out of the forehead to give an unnaturally high appearance to the brow.

Many Oriental women today follow Western fashion and have their naturally straight hair cut and waved. The traditional Japanese hair style required that the hair be perfectly straight and smooth. In her autobiography, *A Daughter of the Samurai*, Etsu Inagaki Sugimoto says that it was her misfortune to have naturally wavy hair—a rarity among the Mongoloid Japanese. In spite of the best efforts of a professional hairdresser, a rainy day would bring out the natural curl. The child felt disgraced when her unruly hair was referred to as being "curly like animal's hair." The aboriginal Ainu, on the other hand, regarded wavy hair as beautiful, and one who had really curly hair was said to be a person having "the hair of the Gods."

The use of cosmetics goes back at least to ancient Egypt and is known throughout the world today. When people wear little or no clothing the entire body may be painted or decorated with various pigments. The Australian aborigines, the pygmies of the Andaman Islands, peoples in various parts of Africa, and many American Indians used various colored clays and vegetable dyes for decorative purposes. Some African women painted their entire bodies with red clay, while some South American Indians painted their bodies black.

The aesthetic interest takes one form that at first appears strange, that is body decoration that sometimes extends to mutilation. Foot binding in old China, head binding among certain Africans and American Indians, the enormous lip plugs worn by the women of the Ubangi tribe in Central Africa, the elongation of the neck by the addition of brass rings among some of the primitive tribes of Burma, are among the best known forms of body mutilation carried on in the name of beauty. Tattooing and cicatrization are widely practiced among peoples who wear little or no clothing. Among some peoples the front teeth are knocked out, or filed to points. Among other peoples the teeth may be blackened as well as filed. In our own society in the not too distant past some unsophisticated persons tried to appear elegant by having one or more perfectly sound teeth covered with gold.

The bodily mutilations of other peoples may not appear so strange to us when we remember that less than a century ago Western women wore wire bustles and took heroic measures to obtain wasp waists. In the nineteen twenties many girls bound their breasts to the point of deformation to obtain the then fashionable boyish look. Today the cult of the breast has reached such a point that "falsies" and uplift brassieres are in high fashion, and surgeons are sometimes called on to implant artificial tissues in women's breasts in the name of beauty. Some Western women resort to face lifting operations or to plastic surgery to reduce a too prominent nose. The Western practices of shaving, haircutting, ear piercing, the plucking of eyebrows, the use of artificial eyelashes, permanent waves, the use of depilatories and electrolysis, and the wearing of spike-heeled and needle-pointed shoes are not far removed from many of the patterns found in less sophisticated cultures. The sailor who gets his arms or chest tattooed and the Western woman of fashion who uses eye shadow and mascara, rouges her cheeks and lips, darkens her eyebrows, and paints her nails should feel right at home in many of the less sophisticated areas of the world.

4. The Language of the Body

Unlike the graphic and plastic arts, music, the dance, drama, and the verbal arts do not require a great amount of leisure or stability of residence. Some of the poorest wandering tribes have rich repertories of tales and songs, and there is no part of the world where these forms of expression are not found. The rhythmic poetry of simple societies is normally sung, and songs are usually accompanied by body movement so that poetry, music, and the dance may form an inextricable unit.

Among nonliterate peoples literary expressions are, or course, verbal and they take the form of myths, legends, tales, poems or songs, proverbs, and riddles. The myth is a sacred tale, and when used in this sense the word myth does not indicate truth or falsity. The function of the myth is not to entertain but to codify, support, or validate the traditional beliefs and customs. Myths provide a cosmology or explanation of the universe and play an important role in the religious system, but they may meet an aesthetic need as well.

Legends are a form of tribal history and serve educational and cohesive functions as well as providing entertainment. Some tales are told to point a moral, others are historical or explanatory, but many stories seem to be told purely for the pleasure of the teller and the listeners. There are tales of gods, culture heroes, ancestors, guardian spirits, tricksters, giants, fairies, and animals who play various roles. The stories furnish relaxation and release. They may transport one into a world in which the weak prevail over the strong, where evil is overcome by good, or where one may identify with gods, heroes, or other favored creatures who do not have to conform to the rigid codes by which ordinary mortals are forced to live.

Proverbs are found almost everywhere in Europe, Asia, Africa, and the Pacific. In Negro Africa proverbs are in constant use. They are used to illustrate, to clarify, to emphasize, to teach, to warn, or to administer a subtle rebuke. They are even used as the basis of court decisions as we use a legal precedent. A lazy boy is told, "A sleeping dog does not catch the hare." When a son proves unworthy of his father one may say, "The lion has begotten a hyena." When an Ashanti was asked why the people did not protest when the king used false weights, the reply was, "One does not rub bottoms with a porcupine." And what overly forward newcomer to a village could miss the point when told, "A stranger's feet are small"?

Riddles are also widely distributed in the Old World though they were generally lacking among American Indians. Many African peoples still make wide use of riddles as diversion, tests of wit, and as a teaching medium. The riddle, like the proverb, may embody a people's philosophy. While our Little Nancy Etticoat is merely a candle that grows shorter as it burns, there is a philosophical note to a similar African riddle that asks, "What is there in the hut that is like a human life?" The answer, "The log that is pushed into the fire," is understandable in terms of the culture. The fire in the African hut does not burn from the middle toward the ends as in a grate but from one end to the other as through the day or night the householder pushes the log further into the fire as it burns.

The poetry of the nonliterate peoples is usually in the form of songs or chants. Such songs are an important form of literary expression all over the world, even among peoples with the simplest cultures. In Negro Africa, songs are often spontaneous and improvised to suit the occasion. Carriers, canoe paddlers, the women pounding their grain, work to the rhythm of their songs. In dances or in group activities the singer may make up the verses to which all respond in chorus.

The use of musical instruments of various kinds is also widespread. Drums, gongs, rattles, and reed pipes are found in many simple cultures. The Maya Indians had drums, trumpets, flutes, and bells of copper, gold, or silver which they tied on legs or wrists. In the Cameroons in Africa there were massive war drums carved from solid blocks of wood. There were ivory call trumpets and war horns in some areas, and drums, harps, xylophones, and lyres were common in many parts of Africa.

Dancing seems to be a cultural universal though it takes many forms. In most simple societies, poetry, music, and the dance are interwoven. The individual may dance alone in the midst of an admiring or envious circle, or there may be highly stylized dances of a single couple or a group. The dance may be an important part of an initiation ceremony, an element in courtship, a part of the preparation for war, an essential element in a religious ceremony, or merely a part of a festive occasion. There may be dances to cause the crops to grow or the cattle to multiply, to exorcise evil spirits, or to insure the dead a safe passage into the next world.

In both the simple and more sophisticated cultures dancing may be a part of the rhythmic movements of work or play that children learn as a matter of course and all ages indulge in. In Bali, a child in arms may be taught the hand movements of the dance before it can walk, and a toddler may be set down to go through a beginning dance routine before it can maintain its balance without help. Dances in many areas assume highly stylized forms that bear little resemblance to dancing as it is usually thought of in the West. Carefully controlled movements of hands, head, and body may be woven into intricate patterns.

Dancing often becomes a part of some wider setting of drama or ceremony, and the dance itself may be a dramatic presentation. Secular drama provided by professionals for the entertainment of spectators seems to be a special development of particular cultures, but participation in dramatic representations is widespread. When the arts are brought together in some ceremonial occasion—with masks, costumes, body painting, music, song, dance, and pantomime —both participants and spectators may be caught up in a profound emotional experience. Such shared experiences serve as a powerful cohesive force contributing to the stability and continuity of the society.

5. The Rhythm of Work and Play

All over the world from the simplest to the most sophisticated societies there is some balance between work and leisure, and some things that are done just for the pleasure of doing. Thus we find in almost all societies periodic relaxation of the rules, holidays, and feast days, festivals, and ceremonies, in which the humdrum chores and the daily routine are set aside. Almost universal is the idea of special feast days when a great abundance of out-of-the-ordinary food or drink is provided. The fact that such feasts may be held ostensibly to validate a marriage or to honor the gods does not alter their function as rewarding events. The Polynesians who grate countless coconuts or who prepare giant taro puddings for a wedding feast do more than fulfill the duties involved in a proper marriage. The meat-hungry tribesman of South Africa fulfills more than his religious duty when he kills a bullock for a feast to honor some ancestral spirit.

A common pattern in many societies provides for a periodic relaxation of the rules of conventional behavior. In some societies this goes to the length of letting down all sex barriers, even to the relaxing of incest taboos. In other societies there may simply be feasting, drinking, or dancing along with some other forms of entertainment. We find a counterpart of such activities in our Halloween parties, masked balls, costume parties, and Mardi Gras. Some societies make provision for ritual teasing and joking, or occasions when buffoonery, ribald tricks or tales, and other such activities are permitted or even encouraged. The jester and the clown are stock characters in many societies. By their uninhibited behavior they provide a vicarious outlet for socially restrained resentments and hostilities.

One widespread aspect of such periods of relaxation is dressing up for the occasion. In almost every society known to us people use special regalia as a part of the escape from the workaday world. Peoples who wear little or no clothing may paint and decorate their bodies for important ceremonies. More sophisticated peoples use ornaments, special dress, and decorations for ceremonial occasions. In former days the Chinese had special ceremonial garments and even the poor were supposed to put on new, or at least freshly washed, clothes for the prolonged New Year's celebration. Western societies today prescribe formal dress for certain occasions and the Chinese pattern of fresh clothes for New Year's is matched by the Western pattern of new finery for the Easter parade.

While many activities serve multiple purposes there are others that fall almost if not entirely within the categories of amusement, relaxation, or entertainment. Games of chance are found from the simplest to the most sophisticated societies and are often associated with wagering and gambling. Games of skill may involve physical prowess, and as such may serve other than recreational purposes. Wrestling, boxing, tugs-of-war, jumping contests, and races of various kinds are found nearly everywhere.

In many societies there are not only contests between individuals or groups, there may also be contests between men and animals or animals may be pitted one against another. In the early days of our own society bear baiting and gander pulling were popular country pastimes. In many societies today animals may be raced with or without riders. Some Africans race their oxen, and greyhound racing is a popular sport in some places in the United States. Horse racing is not only a sport but is also a highly organized business in which bets are placed by many people who never see the horses. Bullfights are important and highly formalized events in Spain and Mexico, and cock fighting is widely distributed over the world.

It is not always easy to distinguish between work and play. Peoples differ in the way in which they perceive situations and even in the same society what is considered work in one context may be regarded as play in another. What is work for the professional performer is recreation for the listener or spectator. To the nonprofessional performer, participation may be recreation. Even the same person may define an activity as work or play depending on the occasion or the context within which the activity occurs. The postman who carries a heavy bag of letters on his rounds is clearly working while the hiker with a pack on his back is having fun. We usually think of hunting, fishing, cycling, or horseback riding as things to do for fun, but to many peoples hunting and fishing are ways of getting food and the horse or the bicycle is simply a means of transportation.

Many of the activities mentioned earlier in this chapter are sources of pleasure, satisfaction, or relaxation, and at times may be carried out solely for the pleasure involved. The songs, dances, drama, stories, and riddles all serve recreational functions even when they are performed for their educational or religious significance. In Australia, riddles play a considerable role in the social life. They are often propounded as little songs describing the thing to be guessed, and the singer may also act out the riddle in pantomime, much as we do charades. Africans, too, propound riddles just for the fun of it, and some American Indians, who had no riddles, found tongue-twisters a popular pastime. The myths, tales, and legends whether told, sung, or dramatized afford to nonliterate peoples the release found in more sophisticated societies by the novel, the magazine, radio and television, the moving picture, the theater, or music hall.

Many Westerners have reported that the American Indians, the Africans, or the South Sea Islanders, especially the men, were lazy because they spent a great deal of time in activities that the Europeans defined as play or recreation. Hunting, fishing, carving, weaving, making baskets, gathering herbs or berries, watching the cattle or sheep, telling stories to the children, preparing for, or engaging in, a ceremony, spending hours in conversation with the other men —all this appears to the Westerner as the laziest kind of existence. Actually, these seemingly pointless activities may be the means of obtaining a livelihood, training the children, and carrying on other tasks necessary to the society. They are the activities which in a more sophisticated setting would be the work of the laborer, the teacher, the artist, the physician, the priest or minister, the soldier, the policeman and the public official.

*But "glory" doesn't mean "a nice knock-down argument,"
Alice objected.*

*When I use a word, Humpty Dumpty said—it means just
what I choose it to mean—neither more nor less.*

LEWIS CARROLL*

6. HOW DO THEY DEFINE IT?

1. From Where We Sit

All societies that we know of have some conception of the human
body, its parts and functions, and all of them have restraints or
prohibitions on certain bodily acts. These accepted patterns are
related to the particular way in which the body's parts and functions
are defined. Eating and drinking, coughing, belching, spitting, the
elimination of body wastes, sex practices, the nursing of infants,
grooming, and bodily contact between persons are variously defined
and regulated. The problems posed by the nature of the human
organism and by the situation given in the natural environment are
essentially the same, but the answers found by men are specific and
varied. Thus, a given act may be considered good manners in one
society, bad manners in a second, and a serious moral offense in a
third, and what is accepted as ordinary behavior in one culture may
be defined as indecent or obscene in another.

Growing out of the differences in their environmental and cultural situations people perceive reality in different ways. We think
it natural and given that there are four cardinal points of direction,
but there are other people who perceive not four but six—in addition to North, South, East, and West they add the directions Up
and Down. And why not?

People in different cultures are pleased, concerned, annoyed, or
embarrassed about different things because they perceive situations

* Lewis Carroll, *Through the Looking Glass and What Alice Found
There* (New York: Random House, Inc., 1946). Special edition, p. 94.

78

in terms of different sets of premises. We are so accustomed to the conventions of our own perceptual world that we lose sight of the fact that such conventions are learned, and that without them our perceptions would not be the same. An American who showed an African village woman a picture postcard of the Empire State Building was startled when the woman exclaimed, "What a beautiful garden!" Not until then did the American become conscious of the basis of his own perception of the picture as that of a tall building. The photograph was not only an interpretation of a three dimensional object in two dimensional terms, but the observer accustomed to photographs had mentally stood on end the picture lying on the table. The African woman had never seen a building higher than the low huts of her native village, and she had never seen a picture or a photograph of any kind. What she saw was an array of rectangles, which she perceived as a well laid-out garden. Children in our culture who are exposed to printing and pictures early learn the conventional clues to the arrangement of lines, shadings, and form. The mother who absent-mindedly straightens the picture book which the baby holds upside down is usually quite unaware that she is teaching the child clues that are a part of our learned behavior.

To ignore the premises underlying perceptions of specific situations often results in failure to establish communication. The Westerner who argues with a "native" about the way the latter treats his wife will get nowhere if the two men perceive "wife" in different terms and have different premises regarding the respective roles of husbands and wives. Almost all human groups that treat other peoples as less than fully human, whether they are of different races, castes, classes, or religions, tend to rationalize that treatment by the premise that others are different from oneself. The white American who would segregate darker people, the Hindu who regards some persons as outcasts or untouchables, the Bantu-speaking African who differentiates "a man and a pygmy," all base their behavior on certain premises about categories of human beings whom they perceive as different from one another and therefore properly treated in different ways.

It is rarely, if ever, true that facts speak for themselves. Meaning is derived only in part from external reality, and "facts" are always perceived in terms of the premises, the categories, and the experiences of the observer. Culture is a device for perceiving the world. It is the lens through which we look and to the extent that

their cultures vary men will perceive the world about them in
different ways.

2. Make Yourself Comfortable

We have seen that people define differently what is food, and
that milk or eggs, blood or caterpillars may be regarded as delicacies
or as revolting substances inducing nausea. But culture, which in
this sense is another way of saying habit, not only defines what one
eats but determines in some measure when and how often one feels
hungry. When a man eats he is reacting to hunger contractions
consequent to certain physiological conditions of his body, but his
precise reactions to these internal stimuli cannot be predicted on
physiological knowledge alone. Whether a healthy adult tends to
feel hungry two, three, or four times a day and the hours at which
these feelings tend to recur is a question not only of physiology but
of culture. We consider it normal to eat three meals a day, but
other peoples may eat two, four, or six times a day. In many simple
societies people may have only one regular meal a day, though usually they take snacks at other times when food is available. In some
of these societies young people are taught that it is childish and
irresponsible not to be able to go for long periods without food
when necessary, though they may eat enormous quantities of food
when it is plentiful.

There are wide differences in other culturally defined aspects of
bodily comfort. There may be some biological bases for differences
in tolerance to heat and cold depending on body build, distribution of fat, degree of pigmentation, number of sweat glands, meta-
bolic rate, or other factors. There seems little doubt, however, that,
regardless of such factors, the degree of discomfort one feels in a
given situation is also related to habit and cultural definition.
Visitors from other countries often find houses in the United States
unbearably hot in winter, and since the advent of air conditioning
many people find our houses uncomfortably cool in summer. Americans who go abroad complain about the cold houses in Britain and
on the Continent, and in many South American countries houses
are cold by United States standards.

All human beings must sleep, yet when and how we sleep is to
some extent culturally determined. The average Westerner would
find a mat spread on the ground, a slatted hammock, or an Indian
charpoy as uncomfortable as he would find the featherbed of his

ancestors. Yet people accustomed to the mat or the hammock may find springs and mattresses equally uncomfortable. When European and American missionaries first opened hospitals in the interior of Central Africa they installed Western type beds only to discover that their patients often preferred to sleep on the floor under the beds. The height of the bed, the softness of a mattress, and the give of the springs frightened them and made sleep impossible. People accustomed to wooden headrests would find our soft pillows uncomfortable.

Individuals vary in the amount of sleep they require, but even within our accepted pattern of six to eight hours for adults the times considered appropriate for sleep are a matter of cultural or subcultural acceptance. The early to bed, early to rise proverb expresses a rural value judgment that still holds in many of the more isolated communities in this country. A person who goes to bed at ten and gets up at six or, better still, one who sleeps from nine to five, may be considered both more industrious and more virtuous than one who sleeps from twelve to eight.

In Western cultures, adults do not spend much of their time seated on the floor. When they rest, read, write, eat, or carry on activities that do not require them to stand they usually sit on chairs, benches, or couches. To sit cross-legged or in a squatting position on the floor for any length of time would be acutely uncomfortable, if not impossible. We would find it equally difficult to sit for very long with our legs straight out in front or on small stools with no backrest. Nor would we find it possible to relax by standing on one leg with the other foot resting on the knee as is common among some of the Nilotic tribes in Africa. Yet in many parts of the world almost all activities take place at floor level or on low platforms with the worker sitting on the floor or on a low stool. Until modern times the Japanese woman worked or visited in a kneeling position or sitting gracefully on her heels. Village women of India perform their household tasks while sitting or squatting on the floor, and there are various other places in the world where people usually sit cross-legged or with their legs folded sidewise or extended straight out in front. People accustomed to such positions would find our chairs or benches uncomfortable.

Closely related to varying ideas of comfort are the culturally patterned responses that people make to particular situations. There is, of course, a physiological basis for such responses as blushing, fainting, impassive control, or hysteria, but the likelihood of the individual's responding to a particular situation with one or the other of these patterns seems to be related in some degree to the cultural expectation. The kind and frequency of the gestures used, the degree to which facial expression reveals emotion, the frequency with which women faint, whether people express religious ecstasy by shouting or going into a trance, and the way in which people react to stress depend in some measure on what their culture at that particular time defines as acceptable ways of responding to certain situations.

Laughing and weeping are to some degree patterned responses. Many Westerners have been puzzled by the behavior of some Orientals who smile under a reproof or who laugh on occasions when such behavior seems incongruous by Western definition. Our patterns of weeping may seem equally incongruous to other peoples. Among many peoples both men and women may shed tears on appropriate occasions regardless of how they may really feel, and in various cultures men may weep as freely as women. In our culture weeping is generally regarded as unmanly, and men are supposed to weep only under the most extreme circumstances. The occasions on which strong men in our culture may weep without shame might appear peculiar to other people. Soldiers may weep over their fallen comrades, and athletes may weep when their team loses a game. Perhaps we feel that being a soldier or an athlete is sufficient validation of one's manhood to make weeping permissible.

There is evidence also that neurotic tendencies may manifest themselves in culturally defined ways. The patterns of running amok in Southeast Asia, Arctic hysteria, and demon possession in East Asia have long been familiar in the literature. More recently, studies have been made of a peculiar manifestation among some of the Indian tribes of Canada in which the victim is believed by himself and others to have turned into a *windigo,* an unnatural creature with an uncontrollable obsession for human flesh. The forms in which these mental and emotional disturbances are manifested seem clearly to be related to the cultural expectation of the areas in which they occur.

3. Mine and Thine

One of the common sources of misunderstanding between Westerners and peoples in the simpler cultures lies in the different ways in which they define ownership and the related ideas of inheritance.

Most Americans are familiar with stories of early European settlers who bought land from the Indians or other peoples they encountered for a few strings of beads or other trifles. What many people do not know is that these transactions often were perceived in entirely different ways by the two parties concerned. In many of the simpler societies of the world there was no concept of the individual's outright ownership of land. Land belonged to the tribe or in some cases to the chief who exercised control over it in the name of the tribe. Individuals, or more often families, were permitted to use the land, and as long as it was used, they had for all practical purposes full ownership, which could be handed down from one generation to another. The moment the land was abandoned or left unused it became available for use by someone else. In many cases no individual, not even the chief, had a right to dispose of land outside the tribe or to confer unlimited rights. When Europeans "bought" such land for trifles they perceived the transaction as outright purchase with unlimited rights. The seller frequently saw the transaction as permission to use in ways acceptable to tribal laws or custom. Each side then saw in the subsequent behavior of the other a breach of faith which neither had intended. They simply defined the situation in entirely different ways, and each party was ignorant of the other's definition.

In some societies gardens and trees may be owned without owning the land on which they grow, much as we may own mineral or timber rights on land that belongs to another. Among the Navaho Indians, for example, fruit trees could be owned by an individual or a family, but if the tree was on land in the possession of someone else the owner of the tree came only at harvest time to claim the fruit. Water resources, timber areas, and patches of salt marsh belonged to all the people. Lands that belonged to a family could not be given away or otherwise disposed of outside the group.

Societies also vary in their practices regarding personal property —clothing, ornaments, tools, household utensils, and the like. Such things may be individually owned. There are many societies in which a woman may own property in her own right, and a husband may not dispose of his wife's property without her consent. In some societies husbands and wives do not inherit property from one another—the property is inherited by their respective families, or a woman's property may be inherited by her daughters and a man's property by his sons. Sometimes a man's property is inherited by his sister's son.

In a number of societies children may have property rights that are fully respected. Among the Navaho, young children owned their own animals though it was understood that use of them was determined by the family's needs. There were other things over which the child had full control. A child who owned a toy had the final decision as to whether he would part with it for a price. He might even be allowed to make the decision as to whether he would go to school or be taken to the hospital when ill.

As Kluckhohn and Leighton point out in their discussion of the Navaho, we operate with certain basic premises and presuppositions regarding property. These premises seem to us so natural and right that it does not occur to us that people in other cultures may operate with different sets of premises. We assume that when a man dies his property should go to his wife and children, that sons and daughters should be treated alike, and that all property should be handled in the same way. Our assumptions rest on the premises that marriage is an arrangement between individuals, that a man's wife and children are his proper heirs, that boys and girls have equal rights, and that property is property.

In another society the inheritance might not go to a man's wife and children but to his sister's children or other relatives on his mother's side, males and females might be treated differently, and different kinds of property might be handled in different ways. These actions would be based on the premises that marriage is an arrangement between families, that physiological paternity is secondary to the sociological responsibility to one's maternal kin, that males and females are not to be equated in such matters as the inheritance of property, and that not all property is owned or bequeathed in the same way.

People in many simple societies exercise rights that correspond somewhat to our copyright of books or musical compositions. Among the North Alaskan Eskimo if a man sold a song he must teach it to the buyer and thereafter the seller could not use it again. Charms also fell into the category of personal property and could be disposed of as one wished. There are many other peoples among whom the individual might own, give away, sell or bequeath at death such property as songs, myths, ceremonies, magic formulas, charms, and medicine bundles.

Among many peoples sexual rights are in some measure regarded as property. As we have already seen, in many African societies the giving of cattle or other bridal payments gave to the husband the right to the child-bearing capacity of the wife. At a man's death his widows were "inherited" by his heirs. The marriage also gave to the man the exclusive right of sexual access to the woman, so that any man who committed adultery with her was guilty of violating the husband's rights. In a number of societies adultery is regarded as a form of theft, the penalty for which is a fine paid to the husband. Among some societies in which wife-lending is regarded as a requirement of hospitality, the question of the husband's rights is quite clear. An Eskimo, or an Arunta of Australia, who would willingly lend his wife on appropriate occasions would be justifiably outraged if the privilege were taken without his permission.

There are many societies in which security and status are not achieved by ownership of goods or gear but in quite different ways. Among the Indians of the Northwest Coast one achieved status not by what one possessed but by what one destroyed or gave away. Each individual tried to outdo his rivals by lavish gifts bestowed upon them or by great feasts at which valuable property was destroyed in the presence of the host's rivals and other guests. Many Americans and Europeans who have accused "natives" of being beggars have overlooked the fact that the whole pattern of a given society might require that anything one owned must be shared—to keep in one's own possession more than one needed while others lacked was shockingly antisocial behavior. The Indian or the African who expected the European freely to share of his abundance might himself freely share anything he owned with the European or with his own people.

Wealth, then, does not always consist in the abundance of one's possessions. In many societies real poverty as defined by the culture may not be a lack of things but the lack of a circle of kin with whom one shares and on whom one can depend in one's own need. A poor man under these circumstances is one who lacks relatives.

4. Mind Your Manners

Because their etiquette is different from ours, peoples from other cultures may appear to us to be lacking in manners. What we are seldom aware of is that such peoples have their own rules that often put to shame our most formal behavior. It is not only the sophisticated Oriental peoples who have elaborate and precise rituals. Some South Sea Islanders, American Indians, and many African peoples have rigid and formal rules of etiquette. Westerners igno-

rant of other cultures can have no conception of the crudities and
vulgarities of which they have been guilty in the eyes of other
peoples.

Whether you do or do not open a gift in the presence of the giver;
whether you should or should not turn the plate over to look at
the maker's symbol on the back; whether you put your coat on
before or after you leave the host's house; whether you eat as
quietly or as noisily as possible; whether you carry on a conversation during a meal; whether you walk in front of or behind a
seated person; whether it is a friendly or an offensive gesture to
put your hand on the arm of the person with whom you are talking
—these and a thousand other questions are matters of cultural
definition. None of them is inherently right or wrong, and none is
good or bad manners except as a society defines it so.

There are certain situations found in every society about which
there are rules of behavior to make life flow smoothly. There are
meetings and partings, entrances and exits. There are occasions
when the privacy of others should be respected, and there are persons, positions, and occasions which call for deference or respect.
There are the giving and receiving of gifts; there are conventions
with respect to food; and there are special occasions calling for
ritual behavior such as births, marriages, deaths, religious services,
and so on. But although the basic idea is the same, the specific rules
vary from one society to another.

All societies have formalized greetings that are ways of establishing contact. When in a strange country it is a good idea to find
out which among a people rate the local equivalent of "Good morn-
ing" or "How do you do?" and which ones may be greeted with the
local version of "Hello" or "Hi." The rules may be tricky, as one
lady missionary found when someone finally told her that for a
month she had been using a greeting considered appropriate only
for men.

Newcomers to other societies are often annoyed by what seem to
be unduly personal questions. There are various societies in which
a common greeting is some version of "Have you eaten?" or "Where
are you going?" There are other societies in which one will be
bombarded with questions about one's age and other matters that
the Westerner regards as his own private affair. Within their proper
context such questions are to be defined as demonstrations of interest and concern to which no precise answer is expected. They are,
as someone has put it, verbal bridges thrown across the social gap

between people coming into fresh contact. Our "How do you do?" is a greeting, not a question, and it calls for a ritual answer, not a recital of one's aches and pains. In the same way, questions about one's age or one's destination call, not for precise information, but for any vague generalization that comes to mind.

Entrances and exits also have their rules. In our society you do not open a closed door without knocking, unless it is your own or one clearly in a public place. Nor do you enter a private house without first being asked to come in. In many societies where various aspects of life are carried on outside people's houses, a stranger does not enter the village without an invitation—at least he doesn't do so if he knows his manners. He stops just at the edge of the village, where he can be seen and heard. He coughs once or twice to attract attention to his presence. He then sits down to wait until the appropriate person approaches to greet him and invite him to enter the village.

Most Westerners consider it bad manners to stare at people, but few of them are aware of the fine points of seeing and not seeing which are a part of the etiquette in many societies. In simple societies in which there is almost no actual physical privacy and in which people wear little if any clothing, there may be the most rigid rules regarding the psychological privacy to which people are entitled. You simply do not look at the things you are not supposed to see.

Patterns of seeing and not seeing may be followed in more sophisticated societies as in Japan, where mixed nude bathing, undressing in the corridors of Pullman cars, and other such patterns seem astonishing to Western eyes. Unexpected visitors to a Japanese home may be ignored by the host as he leaves the room to prepare himself to receive the guests. If the visitors are well mannered they do not "see" the host until the latter returns to the room properly dressed and, for the first time, "sees" his guests. This behavior actually is not too different from the pattern we follow on Pullman cars when well-bred people find it convenient to be looking out the train windows as their fellow passengers climb out of upper berths or make their unkempt ways to the dressing rooms.

In almost all societies there are rituals connected with the giving and receiving of gifts and there are occasions on which gift giving becomes for all practical purposes obligatory. In many societies, hosts present gifts to arriving guests who give gifts in return, or the procedure may be reversed with the guest offering the first gift. In some societies the host goes part way with the departing guest and then presents a final gift. It may be extremely important that a return gift be as good or better than the one received, but under no circumstances should it be given in such a way as to appear to be a payment.

In many parts of the world it is expected that the giver will disparage his gift while the receiver magnifies it. In parts of the Orient the host must depreciate his house, his food, and even his wife while the recipient of the hospitality must speak of his host's honorable house, his honorable food and so on. Among the Thonga of Africa when a man gives a goat he should say, "I give you this hen." The recipient should reply, "It is an ox."

In some societies it is not customary to express verbal thanks for a gift. To do so might imply that the gift was unexpected or that the giver was not in the habit of being generous. Among some African peoples a gift from one's own people, or from master to servant, is taken for granted and no verbal thanks is considered necessary. There are other cultures in which giving to the poor or to religious mendicants is a means of securing merit for oneself. In such societies the recipient of such a gift may bless you, but not thank you. He has, after all, been the means through which you have attained a higher religious status—it is you who should be grateful to him, not the other way around.

We teach our children to say "Thank you" for a gift. In much of the rest of the world the child is taught that gifts must be received with both hands. This is in no sense a grabbing gesture but very definitely one that says, "This gift is so important that it takes both hands to receive it." The giver, too, should use both hands for he is saying, "*You* are so important that even my insignificant gift must be conveyed to you with both hands."

The worst possible thing that one can do in many parts of the world is to give or receive with the left hand, which is the one reserved for dirty or dishonorable tasks. A missionary ruefully confessed that when he first went to India he almost broke up a village church when, in ignorance of their feelings on the matter, he passed the communion plate to an Indian congregation with his left hand. The people felt they had been insulted.

There are few, if any, societies in which the partaking of food is a purely casual and unregulated affair and each society had its own rules for the etiquette regarding food. We consider eating noisily or belching at the table the epitome of bad manners, yet in some societies these acts are the proper way to express to your host that you are adequately fed and that you are enjoying the food prepared in your honor.

In a delightful book called *We Chose the Islands,* Sir Arthur Grimble tells a story which illustrates a whole catalogue of mistakes that may make a Westerner appear boorish in the eyes of other peoples. As a young official in the Gilbert Islands he went to call on a village elder. The old man was away, but his seven-year-old granddaughter, wearing nothing but a wreath of flowers in her hair, greeted the guest. She brought a fresh coconut which she presented to him with both hands as she murmured, "You shall be blessed."

The young man took the coconut with one hand, drank the milk, and returned the shell with a casual "Thank you." The child was obviously shocked and, on being pressed for an explanation, she told all. He should have taken the nut from her with both hands, while repeating after her the phrase, "You shall be blessed." He should then have returned the nut to her to urge her to take the first sip. When it was returned to him he should have said, "Blessings and peace," after which he might drink all of the rest. He should then have returned the empty shell with both hands. Worst of all, the child told him, was his failure to belch loudly after he had drunk the milk. "How could I know when you did not belch," she said, "how *could* I know that my food was sweet to you?"

Many societies have various formalized ways of showing respect to superiors, elders, dignitaries, chiefs, or kings. In our own society men show respect by removing their hats in the presence of ladies, when the flag goes by, when the national anthem is played, during a prayer, and at funerals. Gentlemen are expected to stand when a lady enters the room, and children and young people show their respect to older and more distinguished people by standing. In many other parts of the world the sentiment of respect may be shown by keeping your head lower than that of the more important person.

One of the commonest ways of showing respect is by the use of titles or honorific forms of speech. In America the use of first names has become common for all ages and at all levels, but in an earlier day the first name was used to designate children, servants, or other persons of inferior status. When each person used the first name of the other it implied equality as well as familiarity. In some languages, pronouns of address may indicate the relative statuses of the person involved, as in the French *tu* and *vous* or in the use of first names, when both persons use the familiar term, implying intimacy or equality; when the familiar term is the prerogative of one person but not the other, inequality of status is affirmed in the usage.

A large number of societies have elaborate forms of speech, generally described as "polite forms," that are rigidly prescribed and are obligatory for persons in certain categories. Such forms always imply dignity and reserve in behavior. In the presence of a relative with whom he uses polite form, an individual must always be grave and formal. No profanity, coarse jokes, or allusions to sex should be indulged in and if a third person used such talk or behavior in the presence of the related persons, both of them would be extremely embarrassed.

In many societies personal dignity, or "face," is of the utmost importance to the individual, and the essence of bad manners is to cause someone else to lose face. You should not ask people questions that it would be embarrassing to answer. If you ask a question the correct answer to which might be embarrassing or unpleasant, you are likely to get an evasive if not "untruthful" answer. In many African societies you should not give a direct reproof, certainly not in the presence of other people. You may quote an appropriate proverb which will get the point across without loss of face to anyone.

5. The Clean and the Unclean

People in the simpler cultures vary individually and collectively in their standards of cleanliness and order, just as they do in and among the more sophisticated societies. They also vary in their definitions of what is clean and unclean. Many of the so-called primitive peoples are meticulous in their standards though their concepts of cleanliness may be strange to us. It must be remembered, of course, that a knowledge of germs and modern concepts of sanitation are relatively recent developments, and many of the practices of other people that are offensive to Westerners grow out of differences in the definition of the properties of various substances. A particular substance may be regarded as filthy by one people while some other group may think of the same substance as a curative or purifying agent. Many of the practices of other people which now seem repulsive to us were common among our own ancestors.

We regard spitting as a vulgar and unhygienic habit—done deliberately in the presence of others, it is a gesture of contempt. In various African societies it may express a benediction, or a curse. It may be a sign of deep gratitude, a form of greeting between relatives, or a sacramental act. Among the Chaga the meaning of spitting depended on the circumstances. For a grown-up to spit in anger at his father or father's brother was considered a serious sin and required atonement with a sacrifice. Under different circumstances, it was a way of appealing to the gods. A sick child accompanied by his mother and other relatives took beer to his mother's brother who would offer a libation to the child's maternal ancestors. He would anoint the child with butter and spit into its outstretched hands while uttering prayers and blessings.

These patterns are likely to arouse disgust in Westerners, but a great deal of our feeling apparently lies in the connotation of the words and in our definition of particular gestures. We find it amusing when an advertisement shows a picture of a drooling infant, and we speak of particularly attractive foods as making our mouths water. We use spittle to moisten postage stamps, and who has not seen a mother moisten her handkerchief at her lips to wipe a smudge off junior's face? In pioneer days in this country, it was common for a mother to chew meat or other food for her baby, then transfer it to the child's mouth from her own.

There are other peoples who find some of our activities as revolting as we find theirs. To the Thonga of South Africa, kissing was unknown. When they first saw one European kiss another, they were both shocked and amused. They referred to the Europeans as "people who eat one another's saliva."

Attitudes toward body wastes vary from fussy distaste to a belief that such substances may possess magical or curative powers. Many people in the simpler societies regard any product excreted, expelled from, or cut off the body as material that can be used for sorcery or black magic. Any body wastes, hair, or nail parings must be carefully hidden or buried lest they fall into the hands of an enemy. In many areas of the Orient, human excrement is widely used as fertilizer, and the gathering of the "night soil" is an important means of renewing the land. Among some of the peoples who live in extremely limited environments human urine is put to practical or curative uses. Among people to whom cattle are sacred or nearly so the animal wastes may be regarded both as practically useful and as having curative powers.

6. All the Sexes

All societies distinguish in some way between males and females, and apparently all societies have concepts of masculinity and femininity. These concepts may be thought of on three levels; those that are directly related to the biological differences in the sexes, those that bear a more or less reasonably derived relationship to biological differences, and those that are purely arbitrary.

There are, of course, some things that distinguish males from females in any society. These differences have to do with anatomy and physiology and are of the same nature everywhere. Everywhere it is woman's role to bear children, and only she can feed them at the breast. The requirements of child-bearing and the nursing of infants are quite enough to have led the great majority of societies of the world to assign to women the tasks that can be done while fulfilling the child-bearing and nurturing role. It does not follow that there are necessarily any biological or physiological factors that make women better equipped than men to cook, clean, sew, or do other household tasks, including the care of the children who are no longer dependent on the woman's breast for food.

Many of the roles which one society or another may classify as masculine or feminine seem to be purely arbitrary, and bear no relationship to biological or physiological maleness or femaleness. As we have already seen, what is man's work in one society may be woman's work in another, and what is considered masculine dress or masculine taste or masculine temperament may be in each case defined as feminine by some other society or even by the same society at different periods in its history.

It seems clear that in modern industrial societies sex-typed behavior plays a lesser role than in the majority of simple societies. In Western societies only the actual child-bearing role is left as the woman's exclusive domain and most women give only a minor segment of their adult lives to this role. The greater dependence on cultural rather than biological arrangements tends to level out the nonbiological distinctions between the sexes in the more sophisticated societies.

In many societies, clear-cut sex roles are not only assigned to men and women but such roles may also be assigned to many aspects of nature that are deemed to have masculine or feminine characteristics. Even in our own culture the poet refers to the sun as "he" and the moon as "she." The masculine and feminine principles may be regarded as complementary, as in the Chinese concept of *yang* and *yin,* each representing a constellation of qualities, the former male and the latter female. Everything that exists was thought to be constituted by the interplay of these two forces, and everything possessed in varying degrees the characteristics of each.

There are numerous other peoples who extend the sex dichotomy to various aspects of nature. There may be male and female colors, male and female plants, and the supernaturals are often paired as male and female. Among the North Alaskan Eskimo the north wind is male, the south wind female. Among the Hos, an aboriginal tribe of India, gods are male and female, bows and arrows are married before the hunt, nets and receptacles for fish are married prior to the catch, and each year before the fields are planted the earth is married to the sun.

Whatever the respective roles assigned to men and women in any given society, they are apt to be justified by an assumption of biological fitness or natural aptitude, and there is likely to be considerable pressure on the individual to conform to the role assigned to his or her sex. In some cases the result may be no more serious than the frustration experienced by the woman who must keep house when she would much prefer to be doing jobs defined as man's work, or the equal or greater frustration of the man who would really like to cook and sew and who loathes his job at the office or factory. These rebellions have nothing to do with the essential facts of maleness or femaleness, inasmuch as the definition of housekeeping as feminine and work in an office or factory as masculine is an arbitrary one. The matter becomes more serious when the society places excessive emphasis, as in some American Indian tribes, on the bravery and hardiness of men. In some of these tribes the role of the *berdache,* or transvestite, was recognized and institutionalized. A man might thus openly assume the clothes and occupation of a woman.

Homosexual behavior, which is widely distributed, may be institutionalized or it may be strongly tabooed, tolerated, accepted as usual, or its possibility denied. There is no reason to suppose that sex perversion occurs more commonly among non-Western than among Western peoples, though there seems to be some correlation between social acceptance of sex deviant behavior and the actual occurrence of overt homosexuality. There is in fact no universally applicable definition of perversion in that what one society defines as unnatural or abnormal may be tolerated, freely accepted, and even approved as natural and right in a different society.

Female homosexuality is either less common than male homosexuality, or else less attention is paid to it. In our own society types of behavior that are acceptable between females may be regarded either as queer or at least unmanly between males. Women may kiss one another when they meet, may walk with their arms about each other, and may dance together without exciting comment. For men to engage in such behavior with other men would mark them as queer. Yet there are other cultures in which such contacts between men are considered perfectly normal. In some Arab countries young men may walk hand in hand, and in some Southern and Eastern European countries men may greet one another with a kiss. In some Latin American countries men may greet one another with an embrace that would embarrass North American males. Even the physical distance at which men are comfortable when engaged in conversation may be subject to cultural definition. North American men are often uncomfortable at the degree of physical closeness that seems normal to many Latin Americans. On the other hand, American businessmen in Indonesia have sometimes offended their local counterparts by the thoughtless gesture of placing a hand on the other man's arm.

Many, if not most, societies emphasize sex roles by defining appropriate dress for men and women, and it is significant that the mark of the sex deviate is often the affectation of the clothing appropriate to the opposite sex. What constitutes masculine or feminine garments is, of course, a matter of cultural definition. What is considered masculine dress in Western society today is very different from the curled and powdered wigs, the velvet breeches, and the lace cuffs of an earlier day. Long or short hair, bright or somber colors, skirts or trousers may be defined either as masculine or feminine attire. In some societies, rules forbid the wearing of the clothing of one sex by the other, and there may even be taboos against handling the clothing of the opposite sex. In some African societies a man who as much as touched the skirt of another man's wife could be fined for adultery, and there are a number of societies in which a girl, under no circumstances, would be permitted to wash her brother's clothes.

If there was nothing that men desired more than life, would they not use any possible means of preserving it? And if there was nothing men hated more than death, would they not do anything to escape from danger? Yet there are means of preserving one's life which men will not use, ways of avoiding danger which men will not adopt. Thus it appears that men desire some things more than life, and hate some things more than death.

FROM THE *Works of Mencius* (c. 300 B.C.)*

7. THE SYSTEM OF VALUES

1. The Things that Matter

Every society has a system of values—a set of interrelated ideas, concepts, and practices to which strong sentiments are attached. The word *value* as used here has the common sense meaning of something important to the individual or group concerned. A value, then, is anything—idea, belief, practice, thing—that is important to people for any reason. Further, things can be important to us in a positive or a negative way—we may put it that positive values are the things we are "for," while negative values are the things we are "against."

There is no society known to us in which the people are concerned exclusively with material ends. Prestige, status, pride, family loyalty, love of country, religious beliefs, and what we may call honor, can be and often are values great enough to cause individuals to sacrifice comfort, well-being, and even life itself. On a different level we can say that pride and the opinion of one's neighbors may be of greater importance than mere physical comfort and well-being. The individual who skimps on lunches in order to dress well and the family that lives on meager fare for a week in order to make a good impression with an elaborate party are attesting to

* *The Sacred Writings of the World's Great Religions*, selected and edited by S. E. Frost, Jr. (New York: Perma Giants, 1949), p. 117.

the things we call values, however we may rate the relative merits of the things to which they attach importance.

To Americans, industriousness, thrift, and ambition are positive values. We encourage our children to be competitive, to get ahead, to make money, to acquire possessions. In games and in business alike the aim is to win the game, the trophy, the contract. We go in for labor-saving devices, gadgets, speed, and shortcuts. We think every young couple should set up a home of their own, and we pity the couple who must share their home with a parent, let alone, with other relatives. Actually, of course, not all Americans hold all these values, and those who do may hold other, and at times contradictory, values that affect their ways of behaving. In the main, however, the collective expectation of our society is that these are desirable goals, and the individual, whatever his personal inclination, is under considerable pressure to conform.

But what of other peoples? A Hopi Indian child is taught that he should never push himself forward, never try to win at games, or to get ahead of his playmates. The teacher who admonishes Hopi Indian school children to "see who can get through first," or who organizes competitive games, is asking the children to act in accord with a set of values that is not only foreign but repugnant to them. Such children are shamed and embarrassed when they get ahead of their fellows. The Hopi way is a way of cooperation of man with man and man with nature—competition as we know it is alien to their whole system of values. Among the North Alaskan Eskimo the individual is expected to excel, but not at the expense of others, and he should not be too far ahead of other people or too conspicuous about it. The child who pushes himself forward too quickly is likely to be rebuked by some older person and warned that "Your head is coming up above the others."

There are numerous other differences in values. In the simpler societies, the seller who refuses to sell all her stock, even for an inflated price, may feel an obligation to regular customers, but more often her behavior simply represents a difference in values. If all the baskets, or the mats, or the oranges were sold at once, she would have no place at the market and her day would be ruined. Selling her wares one at a time after much bargaining, she spends the day in contact with her neighbors and friends. In her village there may be no shops, no movies, no radios, or television, no books or newspapers, no cars to drive, nowhere to go. Of what value, then, is the extra money? And where else could one find the stimulation of talk, crowds, banter, and the bargaining except at the market?

Westerners are often puzzled at the reactions of other peoples to an outsider's efforts to better their economic life. When a stock reduction program was developed by government agencies to prevent overgrazing on Navaho lands, many Navaho were outraged rather than grateful. To them large herds were not just sources of meat, wool, or money income, but an evidence of a family's position in the community. A similar conflict developed in East Africa when Europeans tried to persuade the Africans to eliminate scrub animals in favor of fewer but better cattle. To the Westerner, the practical economic factor was paramount. To both the Africans and the Navaho the intangibles of prestige and status which the large herd symbolized were far more important.

One of the greatest differences in the value systems of Americans and those of many other peoples lies in their respective attitudes toward work. In our culture, idleness is deplored and it is considered a virtue to work hard even when there is no economic necessity involved. Many other peoples believe in working only as a means to limited ends—why should they work when their immediate needs are met and there are other, more pleasant things to do?

To Western eyes, many people of other cultures appear totally improvident. If one gets anything, all his kinfolk move in on him until it is gone. Many a missionary has lost patience with some promising young man who allowed himself to become the victim of a horde of importunate relatives. What we have not understood is that the family system is a form of security. Perhaps nobody gets ahead, but nobody starves so long as he has relatives. When a young man marries, it is the appropriate group of relatives who help him get together the bridal payment. If a man dies, a male relative takes over the care of his wife and children. The entire family may work together to give one of their number some special advantage which, of course, carries a corresponding obligation. To store up for your own future when other members of the family are in need would be a shocking denial of the solidarity of the group and of the mutual dependence of its members. The group stands or falls together. What one has, one shares, with the full expectation that when the need arises others will share in their turn.

Peoples everywhere seek to achieve goals which the culture defines as desirable. The difference lies in the status symbols chosen and the goals considered important. Individualism, efficiency, thrift, personal ambition, the accumulation of goods or money, competition for jobs, status, or power—all these values and goals so familiar to us are not only alien but incomprehensible to many of the world's peoples.

2. What's in a Name?

Americans have the pattern of introducing themselves by name to strangers in the expectation that the strangers will respond by giving their own names, and children are often greeted with the question, "What is your name?" We call the roll in school, and in joining an organization, opening an account, or in answering the telephone the giving of one's name is essential and is taken as a matter of course. We also use personal names in address or reference and in introducing people to one another. There are, however, many societies in which any or all of these practices might be resented. The rules are so varied that anyone going into an unfamiliar culture should never ask an individual's name without first making sure that the question will not give offense.

In most societies infants are given personal names, and the conferring of a name is often a religious ceremony analogous to our formal christening or infant baptism. Sometimes a ritual bond is thus established between the child and the person who bestows the name and the latter may be expected to take some degree of responsibility for the child. Among some peoples it is believed that the spirits of persons who die return to earth to be reborn in later generations and the child should be given the name of the ancestor he reincarnates. A diviner or some other person may recite the names of the ancestors until the child smiles, sneezes, or cries, thus indicating the ancestor reborn in him, whose name he will bear. Among some tribes the ancestral name thus given at birth is sacred and therefore must be treated with respect. In parts of Africa the name given at birth is a secret name and it would be dangerous to let it be known. One's name is a part of one's person, and a stranger who learns one's name thereby gains power to work evil magic. Given these varied beliefs it is not surprising that there are many societies in which a person should never speak his own name and it should never be spoken in his presence.

The use of one's name may also be interpreted as an act of familiarity, and in societies where formal behavior or avoidance between relatives is practiced, such persons avoid uttering one another's names. Among the Crow Indians the relationship between a man and his wife's mother was so formal that they should neither speak to nor look at one another. The man had not only never to utter his mother-in-law's name but to avoid any common word that formed a part of her name.

We take it for granted that a child should take the father's surname, but there are societies in which either or both parental names may be used, and in some societies surnames are not used at all. There are other societies in which parents take the name of the child. In this practice, known as *teknonymy,* the names of the parents are no longer used after the birth of a child—instead, the parents are referred to as the mother or father of so-and-so.

Outsiders may find themselves baffled by practices in which the child may use either parent's name as a surname or by the casual way in which the school child from another culture may change his name. Navaho school children may take European names or they may use as a surname the name of the father, the mother, or the clan. They may later decide to change from one name to another, or to choose the name of some other relative. Employers and teachers have sometimes added to the confusion by substituting for the individual's Navaho name a European name which the Westerner found easier to spell or pronounce. Because names have a different significance in the two cultures, the consistency which the European expects in a name has no importance to the Navaho, unless he has acquired European standards and values.

The name may have other ramifications. In some societies the death of a child may 'be laid to the action of malevolent spirits, and parents who have lost several children may add to the birth name of their next child a derogatory term such as "the slave," so that the spirits will be deceived as to its real identity and worth. In societies where boys are particularly valued, a boy may be given a girl's name and be dressed and treated as a girl. Closely related to this practice is one involving fear that evil consequences will follow expressed approval, and it is therefore a serious offense to praise a baby.

The idea that the name of something is identified with the object itself is widespread and the names of things may become symbols to which there is a strong emotional reaction as successful advertisers, politicians, and evangelists well know. We, along with many other peoples, use euphemisms when referring to many objects or acts.

Death is spoken of as "passing away," and the family pet that is old or injured is "put to sleep." In an earlier period euphemistic terms were given to parts of the body, and excretory or sex acts were referred to by euphemisms, if at all. "Four-letter words" of Anglo-Saxon origin are supposed to be more earthy than their longer equivalents though those that are considered obscene take their obscenity from the connotation which we attach to them. Many other societies taboo certain words for the same reason.

The childhood rhyme to the effect that "Sticks and stones may break my bones but names can never hurt me" falls short of the truth. In our own culture many youngsters quail at being called "chicken" and there are other epithets that are either dreaded or coveted depending on one's particular place in the social scale. There are many other societies in which the names of things are of even greater significance. In some societies the "real" name of the god is so potent that it can be known only to those who have the power to cope with it. The biblical commandment "Thou shalt not take the name of the Lord thy God in vain" would seem a very natural admonition to many of the world's peoples.

3. Who Shocks Whom

Peoples everywhere have a sense of what is decent and indecent, modest and immodest, proper and shameful, with reference to the human body and its functions. Almost always there is some concept of obscenity. The kinds of behavior that induce shame or disapproval vary but we may put into this category any word, gesture, or act that is sexually stimulating outside a socially approved context, or that suggests sexual behavior which the society defines as wrong. Such behavior is defined relative to time, place, and circumstances, and also in terms of the way in which a given people perceive it.

Not only do the approved contexts vary but each society, and often each of a number of specific subgroups within a given society, has its own set of signals and cues that are defined as suggestive or sexually stimulating. These cues may consist of words, gestures, the use of perfumes or cosmetics, the clothing worn, the part of the body exposed or emphasized, or simply the individual's appearance at a given time or place or under given circumstances. Thus what is considered sexually stimulating in one society or group may be regarded indifferently in another.

The problem of defining proper behavior is made more difficult by the fact that in different societies different things are associated together. To the Western mind there is an association between excretory and sex functions, and the exposure of certain areas of the body is defined as sexually stimulating. Other peoples may make quite different definitions and associations. Some peoples who wear little or no clothes, and who would by our standards be considered promiscuous, may be finicky to the point of what we would call prudery about certain body functions, and they may regard with horror certain types of behavior which to us would seem usual and commonplace. In other societies peoples may have no inhibitions about excretory functions but may observe the most rigid sex taboos. The contact of Japanese and Americans following World War II pointed up many sharp differences in the way in which the human body was perceived in the two cultures. The American practice of having the bath and the toilet in the same room, the regarding of the bath as strictly private, and the use of seminude women in advertisements and as entertainment all seemed to the Japanese to be definitely peculiar.

The majority of the world's peoples put some restrictions on the exposure of parts of the body, though the parts concealed are not always the same. In an earlier day women in certain Muslim countries were expected to cover their bodies from the top of the head to the floor in voluminous tent-like garments. A respectable woman would never have been seen outside the private rooms of her own house, and the only males a woman would ever see were her husband and her own closest relatives. Husbands and wives never attended social affairs together, a woman never received her husband's male guests, and women were not permitted to receive medical attention from male physicians.

At the other extreme are some of the simple societies in which both males and females may go almost completely unclothed. Yet even in these societies there may be rigid rules as to proper behavior. Among the Kwoma of New Guinea both men and women were nude but they had strict codes regarding modesty. The Kwoma girl carried about with her a net bag that hung from her forehead down her back almost to her knees. The bag was for carrying things, but she never left the hamlet without it and she took care never to bend over in the presence of men unless she had it on. A properly modest girl always sat with her legs straight out in front and close together. Moreover, she was entitled to a rigidly enforced psychological privacy and any man or boy caught staring at a woman's body was severely punished.

In many societies of the world women may leave the upper part of the body exposed without shame or embarrassment and a woman's breasts are not of erotic interest to men. In the early 1950's a minor furor was created in England when the *Straits Times Annual* printed a photograph of the British Commissioner General of Southeast Asia walking hand in hand with two young women, relatives of a chief, on their way to an official reception in Borneo. The picture was considered shocking because the girls' breasts were bare, though they had considerably more of their bodies covered than many girls who are photographed on European and American beaches. They were, moreover, obviously quite unself-conscious about their bodies. More recently, a dance group from West Africa created a mild flurry in New York by insisting that they be allowed to perform the dance with bare breasts as they would in their own country.

Many European and American women wear low-cut dresses that expose the back to the waistline and leave the shoulders and much of the breasts bare. These same women may have been shocked the first time they saw a Chinese woman with her narrow skirt slit on each side to expose several inches of her thighs. But the modest Chinese woman would wear a high collar to cover her neck, and she would never have dreamed of exposing the upper part of her body in the extreme décolletage of the Western woman.

To many peoples, the Western practice of kissing, especially in public, is regarded as shocking behavior. Many Japanese were shocked and revolted when they first saw Americans kissing one another goodbye at railway stations. An African polygamist dressed in a loincloth may consider indecent the kiss with which an American missionary husband greets his wife in public, and there are various other peoples who think it indecent for husbands and wives to show any evidence of affection in public or to make any mention of sex.

Peoples differ also in other definitions of private acts. We consider bathing, the elimination of body wastes, and intimate sex contacts as acts which must be performed in private, but eating is almost always a social act. In many parts of the world bathing and the elimination of body wastes are quite casual affairs that do not call for any special privacy. Eating however is a private act in many societies. Many peoples regard eating together as an act of familiarity, and for people who stand in certain relationships to one another eating together would be considered shocking and indecent. A betrothed Trobriand Island couple might sleep together in the bachelor's house without embarrassment or reproach, but the idea of their eating together before the marriage would be shocking to them and to the community.

Reference has already been made to various patterns of avoidance between persons of specified categories. To such persons any violation of prescribed formality of behavior is extremely shocking. A Crow Indian said that white people accused the Indians of immorality but white men spoke freely with their sisters, which no decent Crow would dream of doing. He would not even enter a lodge if his sister were there alone. In many other societies the strongest taboo on behavior was that between brother and sister. There must never be any mention of sex, and no off-color story must ever be told when a brother and sister were both present.

In contrast to these rigid patterns of respect or avoidance are the patterns of privileged familiarity found in many societies, often referred to as "joking relationships," in which the persons involved may joke, tease, and carry on horseplay with one another. In some societies a man treats his sisters and female parallel cousins with great formality and respect, but he can joke roughly with his cross cousins and sisters-in-law. This pattern was found among a number of American Indian societies. To the Indian the white man's easy familiarity with his sisters was shocking; to the white man, the Indian's behavior toward his female "joking relatives" appeared equally indecent.

The social function of these patterns of respect, avoidance, and licensed familiarity is too complex for discussion here. The incidents cited, however, are not isolated cases. Such practices were widely distributed in Africa and Oceania as well as in aboriginal North America.

4. Thou Shalt Not

Westerners frequently assume that the peoples of the simpler cultures are lacking in moral and ethical concepts. Basically, however, their codes and ours have much in common though they may rest on somewhat different premises, and the specific rules may vary enormously. Lying, stealing, violation of the local sex code, and murder are almost universally condemned. The differences lie mainly in the way the in-group is defined, the premises underlying a particular form of behavior, and the time, place, and circumstances involved, but in all societies known to us there is in each of these areas some point at which the society says "Thou shalt not."

Europeans who have had casual contact with people in simple societies sometimes claim that "All these people will lie and steal" but the concept of truth is a complicated one, and there are sometimes other competing values. People may lie in order to deceive the evil spirits or to ward off sorcery. They may tell the truth among themselves but consider any outsider fair game. They may think politeness more important than "honesty," and may therefore tell an employer or a guest what they think he wishes to hear. They may consider "face" more important than fact and act accordingly. They may regard loyalty to family and friends as more important than answering an outsider's impertinent questions, especially if the latter is an official of an alien government that nobody asked to take over in the first place. Every society doubtless has its share of chronic liars, and most people in most places are less than completely honest all the time. But there is no society known to us that does not consider that lying under some circumstances is wrong and that does not have some penalty for people who persistently violate the rules.

A similar situation prevails with reference to theft. The Westerner's experience that leads him to condemn a whole people as thieves usually grows out of the fact that he is an outsider, and therefore fair game. Among many North American Indians in the early days of European settlement, to steal a horse from a fellow tribesman was severely condemned, to steal from an enemy tribe was highly commendable, and to steal from the invading white man was the most commendable of all. The people in such cases were merely following the common pattern of treating the in-group (one's own people) by one set of standards while treating the out-group (strangers or enemies) by another set of standards. Since in many simple societies all outsiders or strangers are regarded as enemies, this pattern made sense in the light of that assumption. Speaking of the Chiricahua Apache, Opler says that theft within the family was unknown because it was unnecessary. Anything one needed could be had for the asking. Theft outside the family but within the group rarely occurred and could always be settled by restitution. The plundering of whites and Indians from other tribes was not considered theft but a legitimate way of getting things.

Is this pattern really so different from the practice we have of observing a special set of standards for the enemy in wartime? The

American soldiers who "liberated" chickens, pigs, or anything else that came to hand in enemy territory, were following the same pattern as the "native" who helps himself to anything a European leaves unattended.

Westerners often regard the sex practices of other peoples as wrong. Premarital sex freedom, seeming promiscuity after marriage, polygamy, concubinage, wife lending, and seemingly unregulated divorce lead many Westerners to assume that complete sexual license prevails. Yet no society is known in which there are not some rules, often quite rigid, regarding sex behavior. Persons brought up in the Judeo-Christian tradition may approach the question of sex from a set of premises that is entirely different from the premises underlying the behavior of most non-Western peoples. The latter are more' likely than not to look on sex in itself as not only natural but one of the good things in life meant to be enjoyed. They regulate it not because they think it is evil but because its expression under certain conditions may endanger other good things valued by the society.

Moreover far from enjoying complete sexual license the people in many simple societies are called upon to observe an unusual number of restraints. While there are a few societies in which incest regulations seem to be the only barriers to sex freedom there are innumerable others in which there are not only regulations regarding premarital and extramarital relations, but also many periodic restrictions on the married pair. Restrictions on intercourse during a woman's menstrual cycle, pregnancy, and lactation are common, and continence may be required on other occasions. Among the Ashanti of West Africa a man who wished to become a priest of the gods was required to remain continent for three full years, even if he were already married. Among the Thonga of South Africa continence might be required of a whole village when there was serious illness, during a period of mourning, when a village was being moved, during certain hunting expeditions, after killing an enemy, and during certain religious ceremonies.

To Westerners, many other peoples appear to show a shocking lack of regard for human life. In some societies parents may be permitted to decide whether a newborn child shall be allowed to live. Among other peoples, no self-respecting girl would marry a man who had not proved his manhood by bringing in a human head, and among other peoples human beings may be offered as sacrifices to the gods; or a man's widow or a number of slaves may be killed so that they may accompany him into the next world.

Among some groups it was the duty of a son to kill his aging parents before they became feeble.

To most of us such practices appear to be forms of murder, and European governments have generally felt obligated to suppress such practices among the peoples who came under their control. But how do these customs look to the people who practice them? An aboriginal Australian woman who must wander from place to place in search of food and perhaps go for miles to find a water hole cannot carry more than one child. A second child born before its older sibling is able to walk long distances simply cannot be cared for and is therefore sent back to the spirit world to await a more suitable time to be born again. The other occasions in which life is taken also have their justification in native codes. There is no society that does not regard "murder" as wrong. The difference lies in their definitions of what constitutes murder.

When in our own society one individual takes the life of another, we distinguish the act by such categories as involuntary and voluntary manslaughter, justifiable homicide, killing in self-defense, first- and second-degree murder, and so on. The state itself may take life in the form of capital punishment, and the executioner or the police officer who in the line of duty shoots a criminal is not considered a murderer. We award medals to the men who are most successful in killing enemies in wartime and we honor the dead who lose their own lives in an effort to take the lives of their adversaries. Thus, in one set of circumstances, the man who takes a life is a criminal but in a different set of circumstances he is a hero. There are many peoples in the world to whom these particular distinctions are utterly meaningless. Some Eskimos, who readily justified one man's killing another in a quarrel and who considered it a duty to end the lives of one's aged and infirm parents, found it impossible to conceive of wars between villages and tribes. When a European tried to explain to a Melanesian cannibal the large number of casualties in World War I, the cannibal was completely bewildered to learn that the armies fought to kill but that neither side ate the victims—to him, it was both immoral and stupidly wasteful to kill more people than you could or would eat.

In many instances, what the European defines as murder is to native peoples what we would call justifiable homicide, or even capital punishment. To put to death a witch, or someone convicted of sorcery, or to avenge the death of one's relative, falls within their established system of justice. The European's interference in the name of law or government is often something completely alien to the people, and is not only meaningless but lacks any semblance of justice and right in their eyes.

Practices such as cannibalism and head hunting have largely disappeared under European impact but even these practices were seldom, if ever, completely wanton, unregulated taking of human life. The victims were almost always in the category of what we would call wartime enemies, and the actual loss of life was usually minor. Furthermore, the casualness with which Americans accept slaughter on the highways, the frequency of homicide in the United States, the extermination of whole populations by supposedly civilized European states, and the practice of modern warfare that now involves the lives of civilian populations would to many peoples seem to show less regard for human life than is indicated in the practices of infanticide, head hunting, cannibalism, or warfare among the so-called primitives.

It thus appears that in every society, including our own, there are culturally defined situations in which the taking of human life is permitted and sometimes required, and other situations in which it is forbidden. We are likely to be shocked at the permitted situations in other societies while overlooking the comparable situations in our own society.

5. Sorcery and Witchcraft

Sorcery and witchcraft are forms of magic, and as such are usually considered in the discussions of magicoreligious systems. They are discussed here because in many societies they represent major negative values; the heaviest of all negative sanctions are invoked against the witch and the sorcerer.

The phenomena to which we attach the labels sorcery and witchcraft are not the same everywhere, and different investigators have used the terms in different ways. Sorcery in an Australian tribe may differ in many ways from what is called sorcery in an African or in an American Indian tribe. In fact, sorcery may differ from one Indian tribe to another and two African tribes may perceive sorcery or witchcraft in quite different ways. We are thus dealing not with specific institutions widely distributed but with broad categories in which are grouped a number of related customs and patterns. In

every society at some level there is a belief in magical powers used
for ends that the society defines as evil, and it is this broad category
of experience that we shall deal with here.

While the terms *sorcery* and *witchcraft* are often used interchangeably there seems to be some value in maintaining a distinction between the two. Sorcery is usually learned; and it ordinarily
involves manipulation of objects or the reciting of a spell. In many
societies the sorcerer must have something to work with—hair, nail
parings, saliva, blood, sweat, or excreta of the intended victim—or
an image in which pins can be stuck, or a stick or bone to be pointed.
Witchcraft, which is the work of witches (or wizards or warlocks as
male witches may be called) may be unconscious, and the witch is
believed to have the power to injure others without necessarily
performing any specific magical act. In many societies, it is considered quite possible to be a witch without knowing it. Generally
speaking, one learns sorcery and employs it deliberately. The witch
may carry out her diabolical activity deliberately, but the power to
do so may be inherited, or acquired without conscious volition. This
distinction between sorcery and witchcraft is not always clear, and
it is sometimes not possible to tell whether the people themselves
put into one category both forms of black magic, whether the two
forms merge imperceptibly, or whether the observer fails to make a
distinction or confuses one with the other. In a number of societies
in Africa witchcraft is believed to be caused by a witchcraft substance in the body; the presence of this substance in the living is
discovered by oracles or divination and in the dead by cutting into
the body. In some societies, however, the evil actions of witches are
thought to be willed, and according to this belief there is no such
thing as a witch who does not know she is one or who is a witch
against her will.

Witchcraft, whether conscious or not, is almost universally regarded as evil but the line between black and white magic is less
clear in the case of sorcery. It does not help much to say that sorcery
is the deliberate use of magic for evil ends unless we are careful to
define evil ends as the society in question defines them. And this
distinction in itself is not easy to make. Trying to entice the yams
from your neighbor's garden or using magical means to outdo your
rival may be no more than a game which the clever rival counters
with magic of his own. A husband may be expected to use magic to
punish the seducer of his wife or a woman may get "medicine" from
the diviner to turn her husband's eyes away from a rival. When

such actions are carried out within the framework of accepted social patterns they are not antisocial and in the eyes of the society they are not wrong.

In most societies people feel strongly that sorcery is wrong, and when it is directed against the society itself or its accepted social practices, it is condemned almost by definition. Sorcery that kills innocent people is also condemned. On the other hand, an individual may resort to sorcery to redress a wrong, or the society may use it against those who attack its institutions or its way of life— such actions may be either condoned or approved. Whether magic is black, white, or perhaps some shade of gray thus depends on the social definition of evil, the circumstances, and the position of the person making the judgment.

The sorcerer may be a professional and as such is almost universally regarded as evil. However, in some societies sorcery may be performed by any individual who gets suitable material to work with—usually something that has been a part of or in contact with the intended victim—and who knows the proper formula or procedure or who has the right "medicine." In some societies these skills, formulas, or medicines are handed down in families. Sometimes they may be gotten from the diviner, the medicine man, or the so-called witch doctor, though these persons are not generally supposed to supply medicines for antisocial ends.

Both the witch and the sorcerer have often been confused with the ritual specialists variously called medicine men, shamans, priests, diviners, and in Africa often referred to as witch doctors. These ritual specialists vary in their roles and function from one society to another, and the terms are often used interchangeably. There is one point, however, on which almost all careful students agree—the so-called witch doctor of Africa should not be confused with the witch or the sorcerer as the people themselves define the terms. Frank Melland, for many years a British administrator in Northern Rhodesia, says that witchcraft is an abhorrence that all Bantu people loathe and fear. The so-called witch doctor, on the other hand, acts as a medium through which ordinary men seek protection from witchcraft. He is a diviner who, among other duties, finds and sentences witches. Yet both European and American missionaries have often assumed that the witch, the sorcerer, and the diviner or witch doctor are one and the same. Even European colonial governments in Africa for many years failed to make the distinction, and a British ordinance for the suppression of witchcraft imposed penalties on anyone "practicing as a witch-doctor." An early dictionary of the Bantu language gave "witch" and "witch doctor" as alternate translations of the same Bantu word, although Melland reported that never in all his years as a magistrate had he heard an African use the two words interchangeably.

Much of the problem arises because to the educated European there is no such thing as witchcraft, therefore the ritual specialist, whatever he may be called, is assumed to be a charlatan. What this point of view fails to take into account is that to millions of Africans, even today, witchcraft is as real and as threatening as it once was to Europeans and Americans. Such a belief does not disappear because missionaries or government officials scoff at it—even with African Christians it often merely goes underground. It is of the greatest importance that there be a balanced relationship between the fears and anxieties of a society, whatever their source, and the means available for handling them. As long as the belief in witchcraft and sorcery persists the society is under the necessity of finding some way to deal with it. To remove the only means of handling these fears —the ritual specialist—without some adequate substitute is like leaving people with a belief in a literal hell with no corresponding belief in a means of salvation.

It is true that the diviner, like the public functionary anywhere, may sometimes fall below the standards of rectitude expected of persons in positions of trust. But when he tries to smell out the sorcerer or the witch who is causing trouble in the community, or when he provides the means of destroying the antisocial individual, he is acting in his proper role. He is in the eyes of his own people as much a bulwark of law and order as is the detective, the policeman, or the judge in our own society.

6. The Carrot and the Stick

Because the maintenance of the accepted values of a society is important and even to some degree necessary to its existence there is always a set of positive and negative sanctions designed to support the established order. That is, there will be patterned ways by which approval is expressed for those things having positive value to the society and ways in which disapproval is expressed for those things having negative value.

All societies use both the carrot and the stick. The rules of conduct are not only safeguarded by penalties but they are also baited with inducements. The positive sanctions in any society are usually less conspicuous than the negative ones but their role is no less important in maintaining the value system. Human beings are dependent on their fellows, and in every society men strive for the approval of their fellowmen. The rewards come in status, prestige, power, recognition, and privilege, as well as in more material ways. The extra cow given the Zulu mother in recognition of her having brought her daughter to marriage still a virgin and the higher number of cattle given for the virgin bride not only rewarded the individuals involved, but served as general expressions and affirmations of the value placed on a particular kind of behavior on the part of young women. The Chaga woman who bore many children was rewarded with praise names, and the value placed on the role of motherhood was affirmed for all to see and hear. The warrior who comes home with the scalp of an enemy and the hunter who brings home a kill are made to feel their importance, and the value of bravery, skill, and industry are affirmed by the warm praise heaped upon the successful warrior and hunter.

Negative sanctions may be social, legal, and magicoreligious or supernatural. The diffuse power of public opinion expressed as scorn, contempt, or indifference is a powerful means of social control. In a number of the simpler societies, ridicule has been formalized as a satirical sanction—to settle a quarrel Eskimos sometimes resorted to a song duel in which each man sang satirical songs about the other until one or the other of the contestants was literally sung out of camp. In other societies dependence on one's kinspeople or fellow clansmen may serve as a powerful cohesive, and corrective force. The individual who does not carry his share of the load or who is consistently a troublemaker may find himself without aid when he needs it. Among the Ontong Javanese a man who persistently shirked his share of the fishing operations was left out at the distribution of the catch. His lack of fish then got him into trouble with his wife and with the other members of the household. The nature of the economic organization of the community was such that a man literally must conform, get out, or starve.

In sophisticated societies having formalized codes of law the penalties for various forms of illegal behavior are set forth, and there are formal courts and other legal machinery to deal with offenders. In many simple societies custom takes the place of codified law, and there may not be any formal courts or legal machinery. Custom, however, can define very clearly the penalties for specific acts, and it can establish without question who is responsible for carrying out the proper penalty. In some societies the injured individual, his family, or his clan may be expected to see that justice is done and the offender properly punished. Sometimes the chief or king carries out such functions, and in many societies there is a council of elders whose duty it is to hear complaints and pass judgments. There are a number of nonliterate societies generally thought of as primitive that have formal courts in which cases are tried and punishment assessed.

An extremely important factor in social control in most simple societies is the supernatural sanction. This is the belief that certain evils are punished and good behavior rewarded either automatically or as the result of the rewarding or punitive action of gods or spirits. In many simple societies that lack a knowledge of the physical causes of illness the person who becomes ill is thought to be the victim of sorcery or witchcraft or is being punished for some infraction of the rules. A number of societies believe that an adulteress will have a difficult labor, and death in childbirth may be attributed to unconfessed adultery. Numerous peoples believe that incest will be followed by sterility or some loathsome disease. Even such accidents as being struck by lightning or falling from a tree may be regarded as punishment for wrongdoing.

In addition to such more or less automatic punishments there are those that come as the direct intervention of gods or spirits. In many areas of Africa people believe that the ancestral spirits reward and punish their descendants by sending children and cattle to people who behave properly and by making the crops fail and the women and cattle barren of those people who do not behave as they should.

We should not overlook the self-punishment that is a reflection of the society's standards and values, and that operates as guilt or shame. The sense of guilt that leads a criminal to give himself up even when his crime is unknown to others and the "conscience money" sent anonymously to the government or to business concerns are evidence of the sense of guilt as a means of social control. Shame, too, operates as a sanction and may lead the individual to further punish himself. In our own society people are sometimes driven to suicide by shame or disgrace and such suicides were once common in Japan. In the Trobriands, a woman publicly accused of adultery or a young man caught in an incestuous liaison might dive from the top of a palm tree or take poison rather than endure public scandal.

The Westerner's condemnation of certain punitive acts in the simple society may rest on the fact that it was the injured individual or group that meted out the punishment. According to Western values, such acts appear to be taking the law into one's own hands. In many simple societies, however, justice is still largely a personal and direct matter. In the absence of formal courts, officials, and court procedures, or between groups that may consider themselves entities as separate as we regard sovereign states, punitive measures are employed that seem criminal to Western eyes but which the people themselves see simply as justice or recognized law enforcement. In some societies the murder of any member of a family or clan is properly avenged by the group as a whole on the old eye-for-an-eye principle.

Some societies, it may be noted, have a realistic practice which requires the murderer to support the wife and children of the man he killed. The Navaho way of dealing with murder or serious bodily injury was to levy a fine that was turned over to the injured person or his family to compensate for the economic loss suffered. Many African societies had a similar custom. The Western practices of taking the life of the murderer, turning over fines to the state rather than to the injured family, and confinement of the guilty person to a jail where he is fed and cared for or where the state benefits from his labor, do not meet the requirements of justice as many other peoples understand it.

By failing to take into account native beliefs and native conceptions of justice, Westerners in the past did much to break down law and order and to defeat their own purposes as teachers and administrators. Not only did they ignore local values and sanctions, but all too often they did little or nothing to help the people understand the premises underlying Western judicial procedures. As a consequence, the teachers and administrators not only failed to instill respect for law but often left the people completely bewildered by Western actions that in native eyes were senseless if not downright immoral. The results were varied. Often the people merely took pains to conceal from Westerners what really went on. Sometimes the more clever and less scrupulous members of the group took advantage of the situation for their own purposes. At other times the Western procedures served to encourage the very practices they were seeking to suppress. The instances of this sort are almost endless, and no Western government has been guiltless. Government suppression of sorcery in Dobu not only left the Dobuans completely baffled but indeed made the European administration a powerful ally of the native sorcerer. By making sorcery a crime comparable to rape, assault, theft, and murder, the government was in effect confirming the power of sorcery and strengthening Dobuan belief in it.

Many native peoples have been bewildered by the European's punishment of a killing—which to the people may appear a justifiable one—by capital punishment: If you say killing is wrong, how can you justify killing the killer? Even more baffling may be the white man's assumption that when he punishes it is right, but native punishment is wrong. Barton reported that when Americans first came to the Philippines the people of the Kalinga tribe were greatly puzzled at the foreigner's strange sense of justice. The Kalinga had a very clearly worked out system by which one who was killed was avenged by his relatives. The Americans seemed to have a peculiar prejudice against other people's killing or wounding a person, even when this person was no kin of theirs. Furthermore, they had an equally puzzling assumption that they alone had the right to avenge killings, even when the persons so avenged were no kin to them and should, therefore, have been of no concern to them at all.

7. Things Are Not What They Seem

Within all societies there are certain ritual or ceremonial patterns by which values are collectively expressed and affirmed. These ritual procedures serve to create, strengthen, and transmit the sentiments necessary to the society's way of life. These practices can be understood only if they are seen as symbolic procedures that operate in much the same way as the idiomatic expressions of a language. As everyone knows, idiomatic expressions make no sense when taken literally. They simply have to be accepted as meaning what the people who speak the language say they mean. There are in every society ritual practices that can be understood only in this way. These expressive actions take their meaning and value not from anything inherent in the acts themselves but from the emotions they evoke and the social contexts in which they occur. These ritual practices have in common certain characteristics. They are generally expected or even obligatory in given situations; they often occur in crisis situations or in connection with recurring events that are important to the society; they follow prescribed forms that are often formal or dignified; and they express what we feel, or ought to feel, about certain values.

Ritual behavior usually follows a prescribed form. What one says or the way in which he acts does not necessarily represent the way he feels but the way he ought to feel under the circumstances. The forms of greetings we use, the way we express our thanks, the creeds we recite, the songs we sing, the formal prayers we repeat, all are prescribed forms that literally put words in our mouths. When these ritual or ceremonial acts are performed as a group they subordinate self-interest to group activity. Singing, chanting, or repeating in unison creeds, prayers, or other formulas require that each individual yield himself to the rhythm, the tune, the words, or other expression which is in prearranged or prescribed form. Marching, dancing, or clapping in rhythm may serve the same function. All these and numerous other ways serve to subordinate the individual to the group and to strengthen the emotional dispositions that bind the members of the society together.

In most societies, including our own, there are ritual means by which conditions, situations, or events may be altered, reversed, or given a different meaning. Legislatures may stop the clock when the legal hour of adjournment arrives before the completion of legislative business. Likewise a person who is a minor may under some circumstances be declared by court action to be legally of age for certain purposes. Something similar to these legal fictions once occurred in a number of simple societies with reference to the ritual impediment to marriage that exists when two people not actually closely related are yet in forbidden categories of relationship. In many societies large numbers of distantly related or even unrelated persons might be forbidden to one another. Among the Thonga of Africa, when two such persons wished to marry the incest taboo might be removed by a solemn ceremony known as "killing the family tie." A similar ritual found in parts of Melanesia was referred to as "washing out the name." These ceremonies did not change the actual relationship any more than our stopping the clock or declaring a minor to be of age change the time of day or affect the calendar. What they did do was to remove the danger of supernatural punishment by ritually proclaiming a change in the circumstances that otherwise would have brought such punishment about.

Similar ritual procedures are employed in the fictional parenthood involved when a man marries the widow of his deceased brother to

"raise up seed" to the dead man, when women marry other women
to become husbands and fathers, or when the slave woman or concubine bears children for the legal wife. In our own and in many
other societies parents may be provided with children and children
with parents, not through the physical fact of birth, but the ritual
act of adoption. In a number of simple societies there are other such
ritual procedures whereby men become blood brothers or a stranger
becomes a member of the tribe. In the ritual relationship of god-
parent and godchild, the obligations assumed may be very real and
in some societies the same incest prohibitions apply as in actual
genetic relationships.

The use of ceremonial procedures to change the individual's
ritual status is widespread. In our own culture, baptism, confirma-
tion, reception into the church, and similar ceremonies signify a
change in inward as well as outward status. Different religious communities have different procedures by which the ritual specialist is
inducted into office and given power to perform as a religious functionary. Such procedures may involve learning long and complicated
prayers, creeds and chants, various types of purification, and such
ceremonies as anointing with oil, or the laying on of hands. Such
procedures involve more than the kind of learning needed to pass
an examination. They imply change in the ritual status of the
individual as well.

Many peoples have established procedures for changing the ritual
status of a person who has become ritually or ceremonially unclean.
Menstrual blood, anything connected with childbirth or with a
corpse, may produce ritual contamination that can be removed only
by ritual measures of cleansing or purification. The Old Testament
is full of such ritual procedures involving the use of water, oil,
smoke, fire, and blood as purifying agents. Such practices are widespread in the simpler cultures and they exist in attenuated or
symbolical form in all the world religions. The idea of purification
by blood is still found in many of the older Christian hymns and
songs which make reference to such concepts as "a fountain filled
with blood" in which sinners may be washed and "lose all their
guilty stains."

All societies perform these ritual and symbolic acts, and they are
of the greatest importance in keeping alive the sentiments appropriate to agreed upon values. We take our own symbolic procedures
for granted, but we often take the rituals of other peoples literally.
The Christians who partake of the communion bread and wine

accept as a matter of course the symbolism of the words, "This is my body broken for you. . . . This is my blood. . . ." Would these persons see the same symbolism in the Ashanti ritual in which the Paramount Chief places roasted meat upon the stools of his ancestors and repeats the formula, "Here is meat, receive it and eat"?

But, if oxen (and horses) and lions had hands, or could draw with hands and create works of art like those made by men, horses would draw pictures of gods like horses, and oxen of gods like oxen, and they would make the bodies (of their gods) in accordance with the form that each species itself possesses. Aethiopians have gods with snub-noses and black hair, Thracians have gods with grey eyes and red hair.

XENOPHANES OF COLOPHON (c. 530 B.C.)*

8. RELIGION IN CULTURE

1. Man and the Supernatural

Religious beliefs and practices are among the most important and least understood aspects of the cultures of other peoples. Within recent years there has been a growing interest in the world religions, and there are numerous volumes which deal with them either singly or collectively. Most of their sacred writings have been translated into the major languages of literate peoples and since these religions are missionary in varying degrees, many of their adherents are scattered over the world. It has been otherwise with the peoples who lack mosques, temples, churches, and sacred books. Their religions are generally little known and less understood. In an earlier day the religious objects of such peoples were described as idols or fetishes, and to many Westerners the people themselves were simply "heathen." It was not uncommon for early missionaries and travelers to report that a given people they had encountered had no religion.

Although it is difficult to find an excuse for such ignorance today, there are some fairly obvious reasons for such lack of understanding in the past. Many missionaries in their zeal for Christianizing non-Christian peoples, did not consider it important to find out what these peoples already believed or what their religious practices really

* Kathleen Freeman. *Ancilla to the Pre-Socratic Philosophers* (Oxford: Basil Blackwell, 1948), p. 22.

involved. Others, like early students of unfamiliar languages, sought to fit the strange patterns they encountered into already familiar forms.

Another factor that militated against understanding the religions of other peoples was the early preoccupation with the search for the origins of religion. In the latter part of the nineteenth century, anthropologists—who were at that time mainly philosophers or armchair theorists—expected to find the simplest societies exemplifying the earliest forms of religion. Some of these theorists sought the origin of religion in primitive man's response to storms or other spectacular phenomena of nature. Others assumed that early man was unable to distinguish between animate and inanimate objects. Tylor thought that the belief in a soul developed out of man's effort to understand the mystery of sleep, dreams, hallucination, and death. Other theorists sought to understand primitive religion as a product of the social life. Sigmund Freud added the psychoanalytic approach in his still widely read *Totem and Taboo*. All of these theories suffered a common weakness in that none was based on first-hand studies of primitive peoples. Many of them were simply speculations on how such peoples were expected to think and feel.

Many of these early scholars made outstanding contributions not only to the thought of their day but to the foundations on which modern social theories rest. It is no disparagement of their efforts or of the men themselves to point out that in the light of present knowledge many of their theories are not only inadequate but misleading. Their approaches provide useful insights and leads on which to build, but few of these theories as such will stand up under the evidence that detailed investigation of simple societies has produced.

Unfortunately, there have been few attempts to bring the findings of these modern studies into any sort of systematic relationship as far as the light they throw on religion is concerned. There is no modern study of religion in simple societies comparable in scope or significance to Tylor's *Primitive Culture* or Frazer's *The Golden Bough*. Consequently, many current popular notions of the religions of people in simple societies are generalizations based on the concepts of Tylor, Frazer, and Freud, rather than on knowledge obtained from modern first-hand studies.

Another obstacle to an understanding of the religions in the simpler cultures has been the uncritical assumption that these peoples were all "animists." The use of the term animism as a catch-all designation for these diverse religions has served to conceal the general ignorance about the religious systems of particular peoples. Sir Edward Tylor in his *Primitive Culture* defined animism as the "belief in spiritual beings," and he thought that this belief represented not only the earliest form of religion but also its minimum definition. He did not, however, as is generally done today, limit the term either to earlier or simpler cultures. He saw animism as developing from a simple, primitive phase into an elaborate structure which served as the foundation of the more sophisticated world religions, including Christianity, and his "spiritual beings" included everything from elves to the Creator.

Most people who use the word animism today confine the term to the so-called primitives, and generally take it to mean not only a belief in spirits but also the personification of nonhuman aspects of nature either through attributing to them the personal qualities of humans or by making them the dwelling place of spirits. The objection raised here is not to accepting the existence of animistic beliefs but to the common assumption that such beliefs are the same in all simple societies or that they constitute the whole of the religious system of any given people. There are few, if any, peoples that do not have the concept of soul or spirit, and in most of the simpler societies people not only believe that ghosts or spirits exist, but also that inanimate objects have personal qualities or that such objects may be the dwelling places of spirits. But such beliefs not only vary from one society to another, they also constitute only one aspect of any given religious system.

Modern anthropologists have concentrated on detailed, first-hand studies of the religious systems of specific societies, seen always within the total social context. Numerous studies of this kind point clearly to three significant facts concerning religion in simple societies. In the first place the religions in such societies are never really simple but are always complex systems of belief and practice. In the second place, the religions of such societies are not all alike, and there are significant variations from one society to another even in the same general geographic area. Finally, in every case the religion in any particular society is intimately bound up with, and inseparable from, the rest of the social system. Thus, the word animism, however it is defined, should not be used to designate the religion of any given people, much less to label the diverse religious systems found in the simpler societies. To lump together all the peoples of such societies as "animists" is a gross misrepresentation of their varied religious beliefs and practices.

If we define the term broadly enough all the peoples of the world have something that can be called a religion. There are, to be sure, peoples who do not have in their language any single word that can be translated as religion in the sense in which we commonly use the term. But all peoples do have some body of beliefs and some organized way of dealing with those aspects of life that are beyond rational control; that is, a people can be religious without having a special category within which to group the particular kinds of beliefs and practices that we call "religion." Lack of a special word for religion in a language may be indicative not of an absence of religious beliefs and practices but of their all-pervasive nature.

It is customary to define religion in terms of man's relation to the supernatural. Religion has thus to do with those things that are outside and beyond the areas of man's practical control. Religion is also defined in terms of the holy or sacred. The world of experience is conceived of as consisting of two realms, the sacred and the profane. Religion then includes things, persons, times, places, and events that are concerned with these sacred things. Others see religion as everywhere an expression in one form or another of a sense of dependence on a power outside ourselves, a power that can be thought of as a spiritual or moral force. Again religion has been defined simply as a system of beliefs and practices with respect to sacred things.

Any attempt to define religion raises the question of the difference between religion and magic. We have already seen that it is not easy even to separate white magic from black magic. Witchcraft and sorcery, which are almost universally regarded as evil, are a part of religion only in the sense that they are ways of accounting for the evil forces in the world, or in the sense that they are a part of the supernatural. But even if we limit magic only to its beneficent and socially approved aspects, the problem remains.

A generation ago most anthropologists, along with other students of religion, attempted to make a clear distinction between religion and magic. Durkheim drew a distinction primarily in terms of religion's being social, having "a church" which unites its members in the same moral community, while magic is individual and personal—the magician has a clientele, not a church. Malinowski saw any magical act as having an aim that is always clear, straightforward, and definite, while the religious ceremony is not directed toward a subsequent event. To Frazer, magic was the direct coercion of natural forces by man; religion was the propitiation of divinities by the believer. Others have made the distinction primarily on the basis that magic consists of ritual methods by which events can be automatically influenced by supernatural means, whereas religion presupposes the intervention of spiritual beings who can be appealed to, communed with, or worshipped. Thus, magic is manipulative, whereas religion is supplicative. Moreover, religious practices tend to be collective, or at least collectively approved, and they presuppose ends that are approved by the group involved.

Actually, no simple, clear either/or dichotomy of religion and magic is possible. There are many practices that cannot be put wholly in either category. In this case, as in so many others, a continuum and not a dichotomy more nearly fits the facts. At one end of any magicoreligious system are those practices that seem to be clearly magical—witchcraft, sorcery, the evil eye, the hex, the spell, the charm, the lucky number. At the other end are the clearly religious acts of worship, communion, and dedication. In any given system the majority of beliefs and practices can probably be placed somewhere along the line as they approximate one or the other end, but there are many situations in which the two aspects are so interwoven as to make any clear-cut classification impossible. Moreover, if the people involved perceive the situation in religious terms it is to them religious. There is thus no great gain in trying to set up rigid categories that will apply to all magicoreligious systems. The real test is not the form of any particular practice, but what it does for the people involved, the needs it satisfies, and the way in which they perceive it.

It should be remembered, too, that magic is not the exclusive property of nonliterate peoples. We are likely to call the practices we believe in "religious" while labeling magic or superstition those beliefs we do not share. But in one sense a superstition is simply a belief that is not fully shared by the person making the judgment. How would we draw the line between the beliefs that a horseshoe or a four-leaf clover means good luck; a black cat, a broken mirror, or spilled salt bad luck; and the belief that a medal or other religious object has power within itself to produce good or ward off evil? Would we draw the line in the same way if we were considering the practices of the Navaho, the Ashanti, or the Dobuans?

2. The Content of Magicoreligious Systems

The content of all religious systems is similar to the extent that the beliefs relate to the nature of the universe and man's place in it, the nature of supernatural power and how man relates himself to it, the role of the supernatural in the life of the individual and in society, and the nature of good and evil. In all societies there are sacred stories or myths which provide explanations of how human life came to be and how the various practices of the society were instituted. The beliefs validate ritual acts, which are ways of relating to the supernatural, and may prescribe ways of relating to natural phenomena and to the social system itself. The ritual acts in turn reinforce and transmit the beliefs.

There are certain characteristic types of magical or religious phenomena found widely throughout the world. These phenomena may be roughly grouped into four major categories: a belief in impersonal power, sometimes called dynamism and labeled by R. R. Marrett animatism or preanimism; the belief in spiritual beings, the animism of Tylor; polytheism, in which there may be a hierarchy of gods; and monotheism, the belief in one god. Various combinations of some or nearly all of these phenomena form the basis of the magicoreligious systems found throughout the world. There is infinite variety not only in the specific manifestations of each of these phenomena, but also in the possible combinations as well.

Among the aspects of religion found to some degree among all peoples is the concept of impersonal supernatural power. This concept is sometimes referred to by the Melanesian term *mana,* but this is a specialized form found in one area of the world. If it is necessary to use a single term for a class of phenomena that takes varied forms in different areas of the world, the term dynamism is probably to be preferred. This power is a kind of force that has often been likened to electricity. It is a sort of essence, a voltage with which the universe is believed to be charged. It can flow from one thing to another and it can be made to do a variety of things. It is powerful but, like electricity, it is neither good nor bad in itself—it all depends on how it is used. This power is not anthropomorphized; one does not pray to it. It is not in itself a spirit, and it has no will or purpose of its own.

The specific form taken by this concept of impersonal power varies from culture to culture. The power may come from gods or spirits; it may be instilled in an object by correct ritual; or it may simply exist, naturally, where it is. It may be found in persons of high status such as chiefs or kings, in ritual specialists such as priests or shamans, or in animals, such as the eagle or the spider. Almost universally we find that certain objects have been put into the category of the sacred or have become imbued with ritual significance. Simple charms and amulets may be nothing more than a variation of what we think of as "lucky pieces," but some ritual objects such as the diviner's kit of Africa or the medicine bundle of the Plains Indians are more complex and more powerful entities that may involve both power and protection to the owner and danger to other people. They may in fact be dangerous to the owner unless they are handled with the proper ritual precautions.

Images of gods, saints, or other spiritual beings are widely used in some religious communities, almost completely lacking in others. Bones and other relics may be imbued with power or may serve as symbols by which a religious attitude is induced in the believer. Hindu temples are filled with images of gods and goddesses; Muslims and Jews are forbidden to make graven images. Christian groups vary in their views on the use of images and other ritual objects; those that are used are variously interpreted both by the church itself and to some degree by the worshipper, depending on his level of sophistication. The Ashanti of Africa regarded their Golden Stool as the dwelling place of the soul or spirit of the Ashanti nation. The stool was so sacred that it was never allowed to touch the ground, and to sit upon it would have been the worst form of sacrilege.

This concept of impersonal power is closely related to the twin concepts familiar in Judeo-Christian literature as "the holy" and "the ritually unclean," both of which were "sacred" in the sense of being ritually potent. The people of Israel were expressly commanded to distinguish between the clean and the unclean. Ritually charged objects were tabooed or forbidden to unauthorized persons. An ordinary person who touched such objects became ritually unclean or in a state of ritual danger, and thus dangerous to other people unless and until ritually purified. In extreme cases the touching of a forbidden object might be fatal. The prohibitions laid on the children of Israel with reference to corpses, mothers after childbirth, or menstruating women, would have sounded entirely familiar to most Polynesians and to the people in many other cultures.

The classic example of this sort of taboo is found in the Biblical story of the Ark of the Covenant. Jehovah had decreed that only properly consecrated persons—in this case Aaron and his sons—might touch the Ark. Once, in the process of moving it, the Ark was shaken and Uzzah, fearful of its safety, put out his hand to steady it. Although the Biblical account reads that "the anger of the Lord was kindled against Uzzah," his death has all the earmarks of the kind of automatic penalty that comes of touching a live wire —one's motive in such a case has nothing to do with the penalty. There are other Biblical instances of sacred objects being "dangerous." A Melanesian would know at once that they had too much *mana* to be safe for an ordinary person to touch.

As varied as these concepts are in their particulars they are one in their recognition of the existence of impersonal power and the danger that lies in its improper use. While we are likely to label these manifestations as magical—that is, to us, merely superstitious —to other peoples such phenomena may belong in the category of religion. When the believed-in power is treated with respect, it plays an important role in the regulation of both individual and group behaviors.

Among many peoples in the simpler societies the entire universe is peopled with spirits of various kinds. The belief that human beings live on after death in the form of spirits is widespread, though the belief in a heaven or hell where people are rewarded or punished for their deeds on earth is not common to most of the world. Many peoples are vague about what happens to the spirits of the dead, and one may find contradictory beliefs held within a group, or even by one person. Edwin Smith says that Africans have told him, almost in the same breath, that the dead have gone to the great village under the earth, to some far country, that they are in the forest, that they wander about in the guise of animals, that they are "gone to God," and that they return reborn in some infant. These seeming inconsistencies may trouble us less if we remember that most Christians are very vague about what happens after death, and that Christians may speak of their departed loved ones as being near them, as being in heaven, and as being resurrected at the Day of Judgment. These same persons may put flowers on a grave that has a headstone marked "Rest in Peace."

A belief in a god or gods can and does coexist with ideas of impersonal power and with beliefs in the existence of lesser spiritual beings. In many religious systems the gods are thought to have very human qualities—they may be capricious, jealous, petty, or vindictive. There is, however, no justification for holding that the religions of the simpler cultures are always lacking in ethical content. Religion does not necessarily make people "good," however the term good is defined, but it may be a powerful support to sanctioned behavior and a restraining threat to those who would do evil.

The concept of a Creator or High God is widespread, but he is often only the first among numerous lesser gods. Tylor thought that the idea of a Supreme Being arose from a preceding polytheism and an earlier soul concept. This so-called developmental theory was challenged by the proponents of a "degenerative" theory which held that the original religion revolved around the worship of a High God which later, in some parts of the world, degenerated into a belief in ghosts, spirits, and lesser gods. There is no objective evidence to support either of these views or to suggest that all religions once had a common origin or that they have followed a necessary evolutionary sequence. It is now generally accepted that the concept of monotheism is a relatively late development in man's history.

3. Ways of Relating to the Supernatural

If religion is to perform its social function, men must have faith in its truth, its efficacy, and its power. Different peoples have made use of different forms of validation for their beliefs and practices, and they have used various ways of relating to the supernatural.

One of the commonest ways of validating the faith lies in myth—the stories of how the rules were established, the patterns laid down. Almost all peoples have some account of how the world began, and of how their various institutions came into being. Myths are symbolic expressions of social values that relate present-day practices to beliefs and events in the distant past. Myth is the charter of belief. It helps maintain the society by giving continuity and meaning to its established patterns. As Malinowski points out, the function of myth is not to explain but to vouch for, not to satisfy curiosity but to give confidence. A myth often carries both promise and warning, and is thus an effective means of social control. In countless societies the elders relate stories that in one form or another correspond to the Judeo-Christian's "In the beginning, God. . . ." The

Australian elders tell their children of the World Dawn when the Dawn Beings went about making waterholes and establishing totem centers. The Hopi Indian child is told stories of the Kachinas and how they once saved the ancestors of the present-day Hopi from devastating drought; the Navaho justify the specific form of a particular ceremony by saying that the Holy People did it that way in the first place.

Throughout Negro Africa there are accounts of a creator who is variously described as the Moulder, the Maker, Constructor of Things, Owner of All, or Master of Destiny. The Creator in Africa and in a number of other places in the world may take little interest in present-day affairs, and may seldom, if ever, be prayed to or worshipped. But even when such high gods are not actually worshipped they may be important to the society's well-being. The honor accorded them and the creative powers ascribed to them serve to validate social codes that are thus associated with the beginning of the world itself.

Among many peoples, beliefs and practices are validated by the ancestral spirits who not only established the practices but who can still be counted on for continued guidance. Religious beliefs may be validated by the inner experience of the worshipper, through the medium of dreams, visions, trances, or the "heart strangely warmed." They may also be validated by the professed or observed experience of one's fellow believers or by the religious functionary. Woodland and Plains Indians deliberately went out to a lonely spot in order to obtain a revelation. For the Crow Indian the normal procedure was to go into solitude, fast and thirst for four days, and supplicate the spirits to take pity on the sufferer. A Crow often cut off part of a finger of his left hand or in some other way mortified his flesh by way of arousing supernatural pity. The power thus achieved became a validating experience not only for the individual but for others who heard of or witnessed the manifestation of power.

The great world religions are validated to their devotees by the life and teachings of the founders, in which a miraculous birth or supernatural powers may be included. There may also have been supernatural revelations or visitations to their teachers or prophets. Such teachings and revelations ultimately become embodied in sacred books, which then become the charter of belief as well as the guide of the faithful.

Almost all religious communities have some sort of ritual spe-

cialist or religious functionary whose business it is to manipulate
the supernatural or to approach the gods or spirits on behalf of the
people. There may be hierarchies of functionaries who hold varying
ranks and perform different functions. In some societies the head of
an extended family, lineage, or clan may perform a priestly role.
As we have seen ritual specialists in simple societies are variously
known as shamans, priests, diviners, rainmakers, medicine men, and
sometimes by such unfortunate and misleading terms as magicians
or witch-doctors. Ritual specialists, whatever they may be called,
frequently have as one of their chief functions the protection of
the society against witchcraft and sorcery. They may also have many
other duties, but they almost all have in common the obligation to
use their powers for socially useful ends as the society defines them.

The will or design of the spirits or gods may be sought in various
ways. The oracle, the ordeal, and other forms of divination similar
to those familiar to us in Greek or Roman history are common in
many of the simple societies today. Among many peoples there
are professional diviners who inspect the entrails or bones of animals or cast small bones, shells, or seeds and interpret the pattern
into which they fall. In other areas, conjuring is used by the shaman
or other specialist. The spirits may speak to or in the presence of
the shaman or there may be a form of possession in which the
spirit speaks through the individual, who is in a trancelike state.

In many parts of the world petitioners must put themselves in
proper ritual condition to make contact with the gods or spirits.
Such ritual acts of preparation may be comparable to the inward
preparation that Christians are supposed to make before partaking
of the sacramental bread and wine, or they may approximate the
rituals of confession, penance, and absolution. Fasting is a widespread form of ritual preparation and there are societies in which
the individual is subjected to induced vomiting or purging as forms
of purification. There may be sweat baths, ritual washing such as the
foot-washing ceremonies of some Christian sects, sprinkling with
holy water, anointing with oil, the laying on of hands, or the reciting of ritual formulas. Prayers may be in the form of petition,
admonition, or adoration. The approach in an ancestral cult may
be made by the head of the family on its behalf. There may be
regularly established times and places for worshippers to gather,
as in a church or synagogue. The worshipper may manipulate
sacred objects, such as a rosary or prayer wheel, to assist him in his
approach to his god.

Special dress or decoration of the body may be required for approach to the supernatural. In many simple societies the body may be painted or decorated to indicate one's ritual condition, and the use of masks in magicoreligious ceremonies is found almost all over the world. In our own culture Jews, Catholics, and some Protestants use robes, caps, or prayer shawls in religious services. Some Christian churches require that women cover their heads before entering the church and in some parts of the world people must remove their shoes before entering mosques or temples. Ritual dress is often rich and formal but it may be just the opposite. An Ashanti who approached the place where the sacred stools of his ancestors were stored wore his oldest clothes and on entering the room he bared his shoulder and stepped out of, and on top of, his sandals. The fact that in one religious community the priest dons the finest of ceremonial robes while in another he must approach the spirits dressed in rags is unimportant. The underlying purpose is to mark the occasion in some special way. The same principle underlies posture—bowing, kneeling, standing, or prostrating oneself—during the religious ceremony. Such postures are ritual acts signifying respect or reverence and they take the form deemed appropriate by the culture in which they occur.

Ritual acts renew and strengthen beliefs. When the group as a whole participates in singing, dancing, clapping, or recitation of creeds or prayers, the collective sentiments are strengthened and reinforced by the shared activity. Even when the ritual is performed by the specialist alone the knowledge that proper ceremonies have taken place gives assurance that the powers of the universe have been enlisted on behalf of the group.

4. The Tribal Religions

The more closely the various societies of the world are studied, the more apparent it is that the religions of tribal peoples are always complex systems, that they show striking variations one from another, and that in each case the magicoreligious system is clearly interwoven with the rest of the culture. In such societies, unless introduced from the outside, there are no competing faiths. Religion is never optional; you do not choose it any more than you choose your relatives. The accepted religious beliefs and practices are not only taken for granted, they are learned in the same way that other culture patterns are learned. Such religions are not normally of a proselytizing kind; they are conceived of as inseparable from the total identity of the group of whose life they are a part. Since the religious system is usually coextensive with the tribal grouping itself, we can indicate the relationship of any given religion to the rest of the culture and emphasize the variations from one culture to another by designating these religious systems as Tribal Religions.

We have already seen that almost all magicoreligious systems have certain basic concepts in common, though in various forms and combinations. Beliefs in impersonal power, spiritual beings, gods, and even in a supreme or High God are found in religions which characterize societies at all levels of complexity. Magical procedures may appear more commonly in simple than in the sophisticated societies but these practices are found among the folk in all societies. Belief in the evil eye, notions that one may be bewitched, the belief that sacred objects have power in themselves, the use of charms and amulets, are widespread in European and American culture as well as elsewhere in the world.

The distortion that grows out of treating the religions of the simpler societies as if they were all alike is well illustrated in the differences that can be found in the same general geographic area. Ruth Benedict points up the sharp differences found in the religious systems of North American Indian tribes. She describes the highly formalized systems of the Zuni Indians of the Southwest, among whom religion was always a prescribed group affair and individual approaches to the supernatural were looked on with suspicion. In contrast to these formalized group procedures, the Indians of the Plains received power from personal contact with the supernatural. The young man went out alone to seek a vision and obtain a guardian spirit, often through fasting and self-mutilation. An even more striking contrast is found between the highly elaborate rituals involving human sacrifice which characterized the Aztecs and the almost complete absence of even animal sacrifice among most other North American tribes.

When religion is interwoven with the rest of the culture it is impossible to understand the religious beliefs and practices of the people without some knowledge of the total system with which, in each case, the religion is so intimately bound. Only rarely has the Westerner, whether theologian, missionary, or government official, been trained in the techniques needed to study the social system of another culture. Yet the person who lacks a knowledge of such techniques, regardless of his training in theology or in other areas, really has no handle by which to grasp the problem of religion in the simple society.

5. The World Religions

A large portion of the world's population can be identified, at least nominally, with one or another of the major religions. These religions are far too complex for any extended treatment here and books about them are plentiful and easily available to the general reader. The purpose here is to point up some of the ways in which these faiths differ from the tribal religions, and to indicate something of their significance as major elements in the cultures of numerous peoples.

All of the great religions have become institutionalized. They have churches, temples, synagogues, or mosques in which their devotees gather for worship or teaching. Most of them claim a real or legendary founder, or some charismatic leader, prophet, or teacher who is revered, and sometimes worshipped. All of them have one or more sacred books in which are embodied the sayings or teachings of their founders, prophets, or teachers. In some of these religions a miraculous origin is ascribed to the founder, and the sacred books may be believed to be based on divine revelations. In most of these religions there are special persons such as priests, monks, rabbis, or ministers who carry out prescribed functions and rituals. Some of them have developed elaborate institutionalized structures with whole hierarchies of functionaries who fill various roles.

The world religions differ from the tribal religions also in the fact that there is sometimes, if not usually, the possibility that one may choose or reject membership in the group, though in practice this may not be so. In an area where the religion has become established and where there is no competing religious system, the individual may be said to be born into the religious community with as little opportunity for choice as he would have in a tribal group. In many instances the religious beliefs and practices permeate the whole of life. However, most of these religions have spread beyond their original borders to become competing religions in other areas. Many of them make converts, and some of them are actively missionary.

All of the world religions had their origins in Asia. Southwest

Asia was the birthplace of Zoroastrianism, Judaism, Christianity, and Islam. India gave rise to Hinduism and Buddhism. Confucianism and Taoism had their origins in China. Shinto, which is limited in the main to Japan or to Japanese settlements, is more in the nature of a super-tribal or state religion and is not generally classed as one of the world religions.

The world religions vary in the degree to which they demand the complete and exclusive loyalty of their adherents. Judaism, Christianity, and Islam are exclusive in that each requires of its followers absolute allegiance to the one God, though he is differently interpreted in each case. All three rest on the foundation of the Old Testament, and they share a common reverence for the ancient places of the region known as the Holy Land. All three are monotheistic, though Jews and Muslims regard the Christian doctrine of the Trinity as being less strictly monotheistic than their own conceptions. Each lays claim to be a revealed religion, and each makes ethical demands upon its adherents.

In contrast to these three, the religions having their origin in India or China are highly permissive. Hinduism has absorbed and incorporated many gods. Some Hindus see the millions of gods as separate deities, others look upon them all as aspects of Brahman. Buddhism is aggressively missionary but it is also permissive. It not only exists side by side with Taoism and Confucianism in China and with Shinto in Japan, but one may embrace any or all of them without conflict.

It is important to realize that no one of these religions is a single entity. Christianity not only has its major divisions into Roman Catholicism, the Eastern orthodoxies, Anglicanism, and Protestantism, but within Protestantism the variety of sects and cults runs into the hundreds. Buddhism has its Hinayana and Mahayana divisions, as well as Tibetan Lamaism. Muslims may be Shiites or Sunnis, and Judaism has its Orthodox, Conservative, and Reform groups. Someone has said that Hinduism has so many sects that it seems more like a congress of religions than a single faith.

Moreover there is always a difference in the interpretations and the practices of the educated and sophisticated people and the ignorant masses. Hinduism means one thing to its philosophers, another to its sadhus or holy men, and still other things to its millions of unlettered followers. No religion arrived full-blown as a completely new system. All of them arose out of, or rest upon, either some earlier form or crude folk beliefs and practices which in time the more sophisticated may come to label superstitions. Almost all of the magical practices found today among the tribal religions can be found to some degree among the less sophisticated peoples in the areas supposedly dominated by one of the world religions.

It is also important to note that these religions have taken different forms and have had varied emphases in different periods of history. The teachings of the founder or of the prophets may become formalized, or may be attenuated by priest or ritual. On the other hand, the harsher and cruder teachings of an earlier day may become softened and symbolized into more acceptable forms. There is also a difference in the ideal and the actual. The exalted teachings of the founder or prophet may be given lip service while practice falls far behind. These world religions are sometimes spoken of as the living religions. Perhaps one of the reasons for their enduring quality is the fact that their teachings have lent themselves to adaptation to man's changing life through the ages.

6. The Function of Religion

The religion of any people is best understood in terms of its function; that is, what it means to and does for its adherents, and the part it plays in the total life of the community.

The universality of religion suggests that it is not possible for a society to exist without some form of symbolic solutions to the fundamental problems that confront human beings. People everywhere are faced not only with the social necessities of day-by-day living, but with crises of birth and death, illness, accident, suffering, disappointment, failure, and frustration. There are forces and powers that are both mysterious and beyond rational control. There is drought, flood, pestilence, famine, forest fires, earthquakes, and tidal waves. There are other mysteries that go along with being human. Human beings have the capacity to enjoy beauty and to feel wonder and awe. Man everywhere has the capacity for love and tenderness, for hope and aspiration, for pride and creativity, for unselfishness and self-discipline. But he also has contrary capacities for selfishness and greed, for hostility and envy. He has the power of speech and of abstract thought, and he is a creature who can make and use symbols. In magic and religion he has found an outlet for his needs and desires, and an answer to his hopes and fears.

All magicoreligious systems must take account of the universal problems of evil and suffering. They may treat evil as an illusion or they may make of suffering a moral asset. The religion that does not postulate an all-powerful, moral, and beneficent god usually has some kind of simple answer in the form of evil spirits, ghosts, demons, witches, or devils on whom the responsibility for evil may be laid. In the absence of scientific knowledge of cause and effect, with no modern medical knowledge, and with no god on whose shoulders they can lay the load of both morality and omnipotence, people find in these evil beings scapegoats for tensions and hostility that would otherwise disrupt the society.

There probably have always been religious skeptics but only in the modern world have there been wholesale denials of religion or efforts to establish what may be called secular religions. Until the emergence of communist societies no human groups were known that did not have some kind of system of beliefs and practices that could be called religious. Communism itself has many of the earmarks of a religion or at least of a religion in the making. While communists repudiate the supernatural, they give complete allegiance to a system of beliefs and practices that has many of the characteristics of a magicoreligious system. They have a body of beliefs to which they are completely committed, and they perform rites and ceremonies with a fervor that it is hard to label as anything but religious in its intensity.

Scientific humanism, too, abjures the supernatural. However valid it may appear to the sophisticated, it offers little hope for the world's masses who still seek answers to problems that are beyond their comprehension. As older religious forms lose their appeal, new cults arise to take their places in popular favor. Man's need for assurance and help is attested in the snake-handling cults that flourish in isolated communities, in the popularity of figures like Father Divine, in the "store front" churches of our modern cities, in the rise of groups like the Muslim Brotherhood (generally called the "Black Muslims") and the nativistic cults appealing to the culturally dispossessed. Examples of such cults are found in the Mau Mau, in the various "prophets" which have arisen in Africa and elsewhere, in the Ghost Dance and the Peyote cult among American Indians, and in the Melanesian "cargo cults" in which mysterious ships are expected to arrive laden with supplies to meet all the people's needs and desires.

Even seemingly sophisticated persons may revert to earlier forms of dependence on supernatural aid in times of stress and uncertainty when the forces of nature defy the control of modern science and technology. During the eruption of a Hawaiian volcano in 1960 some highly educated individuals openly sought to appease the volcano goddess *Pele* by ritual acts which included offerings thrown into the lava, the flow of which modern man's technical skill could not halt.

Not all religions are ethical in the sense in which we commonly interpret the term, but all of them represent ways in which people have sought to bring themselves into harmony with the powers of the universe, however those powers may be conceived. Religion, whatever its form, helps to assure man of his place in the world, seen or unseen. It is an expression of his dependence on powers outside himself, and of his obligation to those powers. Although competing religions may be disruptive factors, the opposite has been true in simple societies in which a shared system of beliefs and practices serves as a powerful cohesive force.

There is a common element in all religions in that they all have to do with man's efforts to come to terms with what someone has called the forces that lie beyond the light of his campfires. As in many other aspects of culture different peoples have found different —and in varying degrees satisfactory—answers to universal problems. It is the search itself that testifies to our common humanity and to our common need to come to terms with the powers of the universe that lie outside and beyond ourselves.

If any country in the world could be called the most fortunate recipient of cultural and technical assistance from abroad, America is that country—only at the risk of our souls can we forget that the reason we can be givers to the world now is that we have been takers in the past.

DATUS C. SMITH JR.*

9. THE LONG ROAD

1. Cultural Beginnings

We who are citizens of the United States are apt to think of our country not only as self-made but as generous to a fault in giving to the rest of the world. Actually, we are deeply in debt to other peoples. The plants and animals we use for food, our form of writing, the paper and printing presses that bring us the news of the world, the basic inventions that underlie our technological civilization, even our ethical values and religious concepts were discovered, invented, developed, or thought out by peoples in other times and other places. James Harvey Robinson went so far as to say that except for our animal equipment practically all we have was handed to us gratis, and that civilization itself is little else than getting something for nothing.

Not only do Americans share in this general heritage from the past but we have been beneficiaries in numerous other ways. The early settlers learned from the native Indians many of their adaptive techniques. They followed trails the Indians had blazed; and to this day we use countless place names which the Indians had given to mountains, rivers, and settlements. We owe to the Indians many of our most widely used foods and other products including beans, corn, squash, tomatoes, pumpkins, both white and sweet potatoes, vanilla, tapioca, chocolate, chili, cocaine, and tobacco. Even those ubiquitous and typically American products—peanuts, popcorn, and chewing gum—came from the Indians.

* "American Books Abroad" in *Essential Books*, Vol. I, No. 4, April 1956.

Composers, musicians, and artists from all over the world have enriched our cultural life, while poets, novelists, and essayists have added to the stature of our literature. In the fields of biology, genetics, experimental medicine, and psychiatry our debt is equally great. In the physical sciences we have had the great gifts of such giants as Steinmetz and Einstein, and our casualty lists in any war read like a roster of the United Nations. Our present-day research laboratories, our hospitals, our universities, our concert halls, as well as our ordinary business concerns, all attest the continuing contributions being made by men and women of every race and nation to which America has opened her doors.

America's debt is not merely a debt we acquired as a nation. We also share in the debt owed to others by the whole Western world, for what we know as European, or Western, civilization rests on foundations that were not of Europe's making. As Gordon Childe points out, Western culture is on the main stream only because our cultural tradition has captured and made tributary a larger volume of once parallel traditions. The main stream of modern Western culture flows from Mesopotamia and Egypt through Crete, Greece, Rome, Byzantium, and Islam, thence to Atlantic Europe and America. The stream has, however, been repeatedly swollen by currents flowing into it from India, China, Mexico, and Peru, and from countless other peoples of whom we may never have heard. The stream began with many smaller streams a very long time ago. Therefore, to really understand the modern world's debt to the past we need to go back to man's cultural beginnings.

The long road by which man came to be a fully human creature need not concern us here. We might say that our story begins with man's earliest use of fire and language, though nobody can point to even an approximate date for such beginnings. These things represent the capacity for culture and they bind modern man to his most distant human forebears. As William Howells expresses it, there is, in a way, less difference between Buckingham Palace and a cave with a fire near the entrance than there is between a cave with a fire and a cave in which nobody knows how to make a fire.

Our knowledge of the life of men of the Old Stone Age is necessarily scant and man's conquest of the earth moved slowly, for there was much to learn. Man is a weak and poorly endowed creature as far as his physical body is concerned and his survival depended on the use of his brain and his hands. To compensate for his thin-skinned and furless body and for his lack of powerful teeth, horns, hooves, or sheer body size and strength, he had to discover ways to outwit the physically more powerful animals. He had to invent tools and weapons that would enable him to kill animals larger than himself, to scrape and dress their skins to protect his own body, and to learn to use fire not only for warmth but to cook substances that otherwise would have been inedible. Even the earliest men needed to acquire a considerable astronomical, geological, botanical, and zoological knowledge and to develop some sort of cooperative procedures. Thus even in this early day men were laying the foundations of science and of social organization. And as little by little man added to his store of experience each new generation could build on the knowledge handed down from their elders.

Eight or ten thousand years ago Indians had already reached and settled much of the New World, and people of modern racial types were spread pretty well over the earth—Caucasoids in Europe, North Africa, and Western Asia; Mongoloids in East Asia and the New World; Negroids in Africa and parts of Oceania; Australoids in Australia, and perhaps the southern tip of India. Everywhere men depended on hunting, fishing, and gathering of wild food plants and because such supplies are rarely abundant most peoples of necessity lived in relatively small groups.

Then, probably before 6000 B.C., and perhaps in more than one place, some of these cultural forerunners of ours made the major discovery that food need not be a catch-as-catch-can search. Somewhere in the fertile areas stretching from Egypt to Iran and from Abyssinia to Afghanistan men discovered how to plant and grow their own vegetable foods. Among the wild grasses found in this region were the ancestors of our modern wheat, oats, rye, and barley. Fortunately, these grains could be acclimated to northern environments, though it was to be several thousand years before North Europeans acquired the plants from their more sophisticated neighbors to the Southeast. Other plants domesticated in this region include many of our common fruits and vegetables, such as peas, onions, cucumbers, olives, apples, pears, peaches, plums, dates, and figs. In Southeast Asia other wild plants were domesticated; some of them like taro and breadfruit, are generally unknown to the West. Other plants such as bananas, coconuts, and rice are important elements in our diet today.

Equally important to man's future was the domestication of the animals he had formerly hunted. Probably the first domesticated animal was the dog, which may have assisted in the hunt. Not all animals were domesticated at once, and not all in the same place for the wild species had to be present before it could be tamed and later made to serve man's purposes. Most of our common domestic animals came from Southwest Asia or East Africa—cattle, sheep, goats and donkeys were domesticated there. Pigs may have been domesticated twice, from different wild breeds in Southwest and Southeast Asia. Horses were introduced into Southwest Asia around 3000 b.c., but they were probably domesticated in Central Asia. Humped cattle, camels, and buffalo were added to the list at later dates.

Somewhere, probably also in Southwest Asia, men discovered that they could use the milk from their herds and thus have food and keep the animals, too. The use of unpolished grains (wheat, rye, barley, oats) crushed, boiled, and eaten with milk furnished an important source of food in Southwest Asia, and as porridge or mush has continued as a staple in the European diet until the present. Our breakfast cereals are a modern version of this food pattern. Other milk products such as butter and cheese became an important source of food in many areas where the dairy pattern spread.

The dairy complex, as it is called, did not spread so widely as did the ideas of domestication and the use of animals for meat or as beasts of burden. China, Korea, and Japan did not take up the dairy idea, and even now in these areas milk, butter, and cheese are rarely used by adults unless they have been influenced by Western patterns. Elsewhere in the Old World cows, goats, yaks, camels, and mares came to be milked, and various forms of milk, cheese, and butter became important elements in the diet.

Domesticated animals added to man's food supply in less direct ways. The animals' waste products could be used to fertilize the land, and when men learned to hitch the animals to a plow it became possible to increase the yield of the land as well as the amount one man could cultivate. Used as beasts of burden, animals took the loads from men's backs and heads; used for driving, riding, or as pack animals, they enormously increased man's mobility. He could not only move quickly from one place to another but could transport food and other products from one area to another or from an outlying area to a central village or town.

There is a vast difference between these early animals and the modern cattle bred for meat or milk production, the sheep bred for wool—which the early sheep had little of—and the modern chickens raised for eating and for egg production. Nevertheless our debt to these far off Neolithic farmers is no less. Almost no significant plants or animals have been domesticated in modern times, though many food plants important to the world were not introduced to Europe, Asia, or Africa until after the discovery of America made available to the Old World the numerous plants domesticated by the American Indians.

It is impossible to overestimate the significance of domestication, for until people had a stable food supply there was no chance to settle down in one place or to live in large groups. The search for food of necessity must have occupied much of every adult's time and energy, and there was little opportunity to develop a more complex culture. In most parts of the world game animals were probably not too abundant and human beings had to depend on seeds, roots, berries, nuts, or fruits for the larger part of their food supply. It is doubtful if such foods regularly furnished a nutritional level that enabled people to have much energy left after they met their bare needs of survival. Thus it is possible that the more rapid elaboration of culture in the period known as the Neolithic or New Stone Age was in part a result of better nutrition made possible when the growing of plants and animals provided a stable and more adequate food supply.

The discovery of the uses that could be made of the mineral resources of the earth gave new dimensions to culture. The use of copper and bronze was common in Southwest Asia by 4500 B.C., and the pattern spread slowly northward. Gradually, copper and bronze replaced stone for tools. Bows and arrows, metal tipped spears, hafted knives, and hoes increased man's skill and gave him new controls over his environment.

To us the wheel seems obvious, yet as a practical element in culture it seems to have been invented only once in man's history, and there are people living today whose first sight of a wheel was that on the landing gear on an airplane. Wheels appeared before 3000 B.C. in the Tigris-Euphrates Valley, and later in the Indus Valley and in Egypt. The invention of the wheel made possible a host of new technical developments. The potter's wheel made possible more rapid production of pottery, wheeled carts made for greater speed and heavier loads than were possible with sleds or drags pulled by men or animals. War chariots came to be an important element in the later development of empires. It would be difficult to overestimate the role of the modern descendants of these primitive wheels;

FROM **PRENTICE-HALL, INC.**

ENGLEWOOD CLIFFS
NEW JERSEY 07632

DR JOAN WIDER
ANTHROP   HARVER HALL
ADELPHI UNIV
GARDEN CITY NY 11530

TITLE AND EDITION OF BOOK

UNDERSTANDING OTHER CULTURES   BROWN

DATE

MB KET

Sent with the
compliments of

your

TOTAL
BOOKS

1

COMPL. ☐   DESK ☐

FIELD REPRESENTATIVE

THANK YOU FOR CONSIDERING OUR TEXTS.

PAPER PATENTED BY NCR COMPANY

PRINTED BY THE STANDARD REGISTER COMPANY, U. S. A. STANSET ®

from the tiniest watch to the mightiest engine, our machine-age culture turns with the wheel.

The domestication of plants and animals gave men a stable food supply; the animals plus the wheel gave mobility; and these, along with other developments such as the plow and the loom, made possible specialization and the growth of towns. But until men learned to write, all knowledge had to be passed on by word of mouth, and people could know only what members of the group could carry in their heads. With writing man could accumulate experience, store up knowledge until it was needed, and keep it available from one generation to the next. Picture writing occurred in all three of the great river valleys—the Nile, the Tigris-Euphrates, and the Indus—at about the same time, five or six thousand years ago. Writing was developed in China some two thousand years later.

Thus in the long period before the dawn of written history our cultural forebears, though not necessarily our biological ancestors, had laid the foundation for almost all our present-day activities. Early man had explored and settled almost the whole of the habitable world. He had discovered the use of edible and medicinal plants and had domesticated almost all of our important food plants and farm animals. He had learned how to use animals for driving, pulling, riding, and burden bearing. He had learned how to milk and to make butter and various forms of cheese. He had learned how to use metal to make tools and implements. He had learned to use fire for cooking and heating, and in processing clays and ores. He had learned to spin and weave, to sew, and to make pottery and baskets. He had made a beginning in medicine and surgery, in astronomy, and in mathematics. He had begun to produce artistic paintings and drawings and to develop religious concepts and social organization. Finally, he discovered ways to record his activities and thus move into the period of written history.

2. The Stream of History

With an increased food supply and with animals and wheeled vehicles to bring food from surrounding areas, people came to live closer together and they developed new needs and new ways of meeting them. Inventions bred inventions, and new discoveries and developments came thick and fast. Among the most important of these new developments was the invention of true alphabetic writing, which we owe to a Semitic people. This alphabet, which can be traced back to about 1800 B.C., was carried by the Phoenicians to the Greeks, who improved it still further and adapted it to their own use mainly by the addition of vowel symbols. From this source by various routes have come the alphabets of all Indo-European languages, including our own.

Iron, which seems to have been first smelted and forged around 1700 B.C., provided a cheap material which greatly increased the productivity of the ordinary farmer, herdsman, and carpenter. Trade was speeded up by the use of horses for riding, by the post road systems, and by the invention of coined money. Urban living called for new social controls and there had to be municipal services and some way to support them. Systems of money, credit, a form of banking, taxes, records, public buildings, and the machinery and personnel to handle public affairs became necessary. Improved sailing vessels, time reckoning, new methods of warfare, and new forms of government were developed.

During this period the Hebrews were laying the foundations of the religious heritage we claim today and other religious systems arose with priests and temples. The Ethiopians moved into the orbit of the civilized world; the Cretans developed a sophisticated and literate civilization; and peoples throughout the area pushed forward into new ways of living.

Almost all of the developments we have recounted took place in an area of the world extending from the Eastern end of the Mediterranean to the Indus Valley. But somewhere around 2000 B.C. the Hwang Ho Valley of China was added to the list. Here, rice rather than barley was grown, and silk instead of linen cloth was produced. Although somewhat off the main line of development, China was later to make major contributions to the main stream and to profoundly influence the whole of the Eastern world.

Looking at the known world around 2000 to 500 B.C. we can appreciate the advantages that came to those who were near enough the centers of civilization to profit fully from the exchange of goods and ideas. Within each environment people worked out ways of utilizing their resources and meeting their problems. Different ideas were developed in the different areas, and through interchange became available to all the others. The Babylonians contributed mathematical ideas, the Egyptians invented a solar calendar, the Phoenicians produced an alphabet. The Hittites, who had acquired theology, law, poetry, and scientific concepts from their Mesopotamian neighbors, in turn contributed the process of working iron. As the barbarians on the fringes came into the orbit of the civilized world they first benefited and later made their contribution to the common pool. New languages, new ways of thinking, and new inventions were shared. As Gordon Childe expresses it, currents flowed freely in all directions; in the intervals of peace, the kings of these various nations interchanged ambassadors and wives, presents and deities, physicians and soothsayers.

By 500 B.C. political power and cultural leadership had shifted from the great river valleys to marginal areas that carried on and enlarged upon the earlier civilizations. Athens was at the beginning of her Golden Age. Rome was beginning to emerge, and the Persian power was at its height. From Southwest Asia to China great religious and philosophical contributions were being made. The sacred writings of the Hebrews and the Upanishads in India had appeared. Buddha in India and Confucius in China were laying the foundations of religious and ethical systems that today profoundly influence more than a third of the world's peoples.

When the center of this development was transferred to the Greek mainland, the trade lines extended to the barbarians to the north, along well-marked routes through central Europe. Little, however, was known about these backward areas for a long time. Herodotus, writing in the fifth century B.C., says that the boundaries of Europe are quite unknown. He says, also, that it is reported that the northern parts of Europe are inhabited by one-eyed people and griffins, though he himself refused to believe such tales.

The classical Greek culture, like all other cultures that we know, was deeply in debt to its forerunners. Not only were the Greeks themselves a mixed people—a blend of Aegeans, Cretans, and Indo-European-speaking invaders plus Phoenicians who served as intermediaries between Asia and Europe—but there were few items in classical Greek culture that could not be traced to outside origins. As Linton points out in his *Tree of Culture,* one who digs into the background of Greek culture finds its roots extending far into the past, branching and rebranching to draw upon many different sources. The keen curiosity and analytical attitude of the Greeks enabled them to utilize, combine, and transform these various elements.

The later Hellenistic cultures were even more broadly based since many of the economic and political patterns which they incorporated came to them directly from the Mesopotamian region.

Members of subject communities were recruited for service in the imperial armies under Darius and Xerxes. Indian charioteers, nomad archers and horsemen from Central Asia, and Ethiopians dressed in the skins of leopards and lions, fought side by side with Greek mercenaries and Syrian conscripts. Herodotus, in describing the Persian army which Xerxes led against the Greeks, asks "For was there a nation in all Asia which Xerxes did not bring with him against Greece?" There follows several pages listing the dress, weapons, and physical characteristics of the various peoples who made up this international force.

Through the Hellenistic cultures the patterns garnered from the whole of the civilized world were transmitted to imperial Rome, and thence became a part of the European tradition. As Childe points out, the Roman Empire formed a unique reservoir for the pooling of human experience. It maintained commercial ties not only among its scattered parts but with both the civilized and the barbarian worlds beyond its frontiers. Not only traders, civil servants, and military officers, but soldiers, craftsmen, and slaves were continually moving to and from its remote outposts. Added to these influences were the ambassadors and missionaries sent from the East to Rome and from Rome to various parts of the known world. Not least among the items thus spread far and wide was the Christian religion. Slaves, immigrants, artisans, and merchants carried with them every variety of Oriental cult, but only Christianity provided an international ideology that fitted into the expanding world economy and that appealed equally to the urban dwellers and the barbarian hordes.

With the breakup of the Roman Empire, the center of civilization shifted east. With the rise of the Arabic-Muslim peoples, new centers of culture developed. Byzantium continued the Greek intellectual tradition, and from the East Christianity spread north. Even in the West the main tradition was not lost. There were still clerks, craftsmen, merchants, and priests. The church kept alive not only the dogmas and rites of Christianity but also the techniques of writing and ciphering, a respect for the conventional divisions of time, vestiges of classical art and Roman architecture, and memories of rational medicine and scientific agriculture.

With the spread of the Arabic-Muslim culture, Europe became heir to another rich source of ideas and inventions. Some of these were a continuation of the Hellenistic stream; others were developed or refined in the Muslim culture centers; still others were brought from afar by Arab traders. Among the most significant of these contributions was that of our so-called Arabic numerals which we owe to a Hindu invention of the zero symbol that enables both the number symbol itself and its position to have specific values. Thus 1234 and 4321 have different values because of the position of the symbols. Something of the significance of this invention can be gathered if one tries to add, subtract, or divide with Roman numerals.

Other developments and inventions which had been taking place in East Asia were either introduced to the West or the knowledge of the existence of such developments stimulated similar inventions. Silk had earlier been brought from China and porcelain began to be copied. The compass, gunpowder, paper, and printing with both block and movable type were first invented in China though, in some cases, they were not put to practical use until they reached Europe.

The invention of true paper seems to have been made in China early in the second century A.D., and block printing was developed sometime after 700 A.D. At about the same time paper money was being issued, and by 1050 the Chinese were printing with movable type. Block printing appeared in the West six centuries after it was known in China, and the first type printing in Europe came about 1450, approximately 400 years after the Chinese invention. Whether the Germans learned of printing directly or indirectly from China or whether their achievement represents a separate invention is not entirely certain.

These inventions, added to the long cultural accumulation from earlier periods, opened up vast new possibilities and ushered in the period of European exploration and conquest. The compass made it possible for man to get away from sight of land without danger of being lost on the trackless sea. Gunpowder made possible weapons with which a few Europeans were able to subdue whole native peoples; printing and paper opened the way for the spread of education to ordinary people. Man stood on the brink of a new world.

3. The Laggard Europeans

Where had the Northern and Western Europeans been during all these thousands of years of cultural development? Not one of the basic discoveries on which the whole of civilization rests can be credited to the peoples who were later to become the rulers of the world. The domestication of plants and animals, the wheel, the use of metals, the arch, the calendar, writing, numbering systems, the alphabet, paper, gunpowder, the compass, printing—not one of these was first invented by Europeans though Europeans were sometimes the first to utilize and develop some of the later dis-, coveries. The Northern and Western Europeans in particular were the victims of a time-space handicap, as so many other of the world's peoples have been before and since. The whole of mainland Europe was backward until well after 1000 b.c. when Greece and then Italy were brought into the orbit of the civilized world. Culture spread slowly west to the Iberian peninsula and northward up the Danube, but northern and western Europe, particularly the British Isles, were, as someone has put it, only the margin of a margin.

The story of the later spread of culture throughout Europe is both too complex and too well-known for discussion in these pages. The ferment of the Crusades, the rise and decline of the Holy Roman Empire, the rise of the universities, the Renaissance, the Reformation and Counter-Reformation—all these developments are familiar history, and we recognize them as a part of our cultural heritage. All of them, however, have their roots deep in the past and only slowly, gradually, and very late, did Northern and Western Europe begin to play a significant role in the unfolding drama.

There is no simple explanation as to why a people remain backward for long periods of time and then push into a place of leadership, or why people who have been in the lead fall behind and deteriorate culturally. But the culture history recounted in these pages should give us some clues that are useful in understanding our own and other cultures.

In the first place, race seemingly has nothing to do with culture. The North European Caucasoids showed no slightest sign of cultural leadership until more than five thousand years after the peoples of the great river valleys had evinced their cultural creativity. While it is true that the peoples of North Africa and Southwest Asia fall within the Caucasoid division of mankind, their early creativity was not shared by their kinsmen to the north and west. Moreover, the Indus Valley civilization seems to have been created by a mixed people, and the fourth great cultural center in the Hwang Ho Valley was developed by a Mongoloid people, as were the later independent high cultures in the New World.

A second clue is that isolation and distance from centers of cultural activity seem to play an important role. A number of factors, such as location, climate, soil, and wild plants and animals suitable for domestication may have accounted for the initial lead of the great river valley cultures; but once started, cultural invention seems to be cumulative and may progress with increasing momentum. Ideas and inventions spread out from such centers and the people on the margins are handicapped by being too far away to profit by this activity. Moreover, it is clear from the record that the peoples in neighboring areas of cultural activity stimulate one another and learn from one another.

A third fact is that all of the great river valley civilizations were produced by peoples of mixed ancestry, and both the Greeks and the Romans, as well as the Hellenistic peoples, were a mixture of many tribes and nations. This is not to suggest that such biological mixture is a cause of cultural flowering, although some biologists do see in it the "hybrid vigor" with which we are familiar in the plant world. From a cultural point of view, a more reasonable explanation lies in the fact that when peoples of different groups come together they bring new ideas and new ways of doing things, and the mixture of genes is incidental to the process.

A fourth factor that may have played an important role has to do with the availability and use of energy with which to exploit one's environment. Many areas of the world today are lacking in high-energy foods; that is, those supplying adequate amounts of protein and vitamins. Many areas of the world have always been dependent on protein deficient foods such as rice, maize, yams, and cassava. It is possible that the absence of suitable plants and animals for domestication or the necessary dependence on plant foods that lack adequate protein in relation to calories may have been factors in the lack of cultural creativity in some areas. Man's later technological development seems to have a direct relation to his harnessing of other sources of energy, such as draft animals, the forces of wind and water, mechanical devices such as the lever and the wheel, and the later employment of falling water or high energy fuels such as coal, oil and gas, and nuclear energy.

A fifth fact that emerges is the significance of a favorable cultural climate which in itself may depend on many things. Sometimes a particular development may start or shut off creative activity, but more commonly particular cultural expectations direct interest and attention to certain ends. Thus nations may have periods of flowering in art, music, or other such activities, and then for long periods produce no such works of first order. These developments seem to be more than can be accounted for by the unexplained appearance of genius, for such genius seldom blossoms alone or in an atmosphere alien to it. An Edison, a Beethoven, or an Einstein born into an isolated society or in an earlier age would have undoubtedly stood out among his fellows, but it is inconceivable that any one of them could have made the contributions for which he is known had there not been a suitable cultural setting.

Another element of importance is the time-space factor. During much of man's history, at least from the beginning of the Neolithic to the fifteenth century, A.D., the Mediterranean area extending eastward to India was in an unusually favorable position with reference to geographic location, certain basic natural resources, and readily available communication routes. Northern Europe was at a disadvantage in these respects and, of course, much of the world was entirely beyond the reach of their influence.

Early in the fifteenth century these conditions were altered. Changes in time together with accumulated culture and certain historical events affected the desirability of certain positions in space. With the New World across the Atlantic opening up vast sources of raw materials, land for colonization, and potential new markets, the marginal North Europeans found themselves for the first time in an advantageous position. The passage of time and the accumulated discoveries and inventions made to the south and east of them had turned their one-time disadvantage into an opportunity. Their location with reference to the American continents, their good harbors, and the presence of coal, iron, and water power gave them their chance. Moreover, the new geographical discoveries and other factors which made their position favorable shifted the center of developments so as to throw into a marginal position the very areas which had once held the center of the stage.

Thus Western Europe and the New World have come into places of leadership, but they have built on foundations laid through the centuries by men from other lands and nations. The Industrial Revolution, the building of European empires, the steamships, railroads, automobiles, airplanes, modern factories, the telegraph, telephone, radio, radar, television, the wonders of the nuclear age, and even the conquest of outer space all have roots that lead back through thousands of years and to which many thousands of men and women from all over the world have made their contribution. We stand on the collective shoulders of a large portion of mankind.

4. The Peoples Off the Highways

Because Western peoples today stand in a position of power and leadership throughout the world they have a tendency to feel superior to the peoples who, for one reason or another, have remained on the fringes or who have been outside the main stream of development that has culminated in the Western culture of today. A national news magazine recently referred to the peoples in the interior of New Guinea as being "so primitive that they haven't even invented the wheel." If inventing a wheel—or a system of writing, an alphabet or a calendar—were the criterion used, most of the world, including Europeans and Americans, would still be "primitive." As we have seen, many of these inventions were made only once, the rest of the world doing without until it had a chance to "borrow" the new idea.

No single people has held the center of the stage throughout history, and many of the peoples in areas that are underdeveloped today are the descendants of peoples who in an earlier day were in the forefront of what was then the civilized world. But there were other high civilizations that developed outside the main stream that culminated in Western culture and whose contribution came into the West only indirectly or not at all. As a consequence, many Westerners are ignorant of the long, proud histories of many peoples who were literate, cultivated, and sophisticated when Europe was still in a state of barbarism and America was unknown to the rest of the world, though she had her own proud centers of aboriginal culture.

Longest in the vanguard of civilization were the Chinese who have had an unbroken record for continuity as a great civilized people for nearly four thousand years. The Chinese lost out in technological development in the period of the Industrial Revolution but in many areas their ancient culture surpassed anything known elsewhere and in art, literature, and philosophy their luster remained undimmed. Who knows but from the present turmoil they may emerge as a new power combining their ancient wisdom with a new technology freed of both the strait jacket of Communism and the too heavy hand of tradition.

Other areas of the East have had their days of glory. The Koreans had a long history as a literate and cultivated people before being submerged under alien rule. Japan, while an earlier borrower from both China and Korea, has in recent times forged ahead of her neighbors in modern technological development. India can boast an ancient civilization and great gifts made to the world in an earlier day in religion, philosophy, and science. In Southeast Asia and in some of the islands now comprising Indonesia, civilization spread from India and China. The area is now, for the most part, either Buddhist or Muslim, and its temples and cities attest an ancient glory.

In the New World, the Maya, the Aztec, and the Inca developed sophisticated cultures superior in many ways to the European cultures of their day. They built roads, erected elaborate buildings, did exquisite work in silver, gold, and platinum, wove textiles unmatched to this day, made paper, and developed a calendar. The Maya originated a numbering system involving the independent invention of zero. The development of these centers is the more remarkable in view of the late arrival of the Indians in the Western Hemisphere and the fact that they were off the main highways, separated by the Atlantic and the Pacific from the Old World centers of civilization.

Although the high cultures of Mexico and Peru were exceptions, the American Indians as a whole made remarkable advancement in the face of many handicaps. They arrived from Asia via Bering Strait and began filtering down and across the two continents some fifteen or twenty thousand years ago. They brought the dog with them, but only in a limited area in Peru did they find any sizable animals suitable for domestication. Yet without the aid of animals the Indians had possessed the whole of the hemisphere before the arrival of the Europeans. They had domesticated something like a hundred different plants, many of which furnish us with important staple foods today and which have been carried to various parts of the world. This cultural development was halted by the Europeans who had the advantage of guns, horses, and other domestic animals, along with technical skills and a cultural tradition built on that of the Arabs, the Romans, the Greeks, the Far East, and the ancient river valleys.

Negro Africa is the area in which the lack of cultural creativity has most often been attributed to race. Yet Africa south of the Sahara was cut off from easy contact with the Mediterranean and Near Eastern areas by mountains, deserts, and cataracts in the Nile. The only contact of Europe with the Negro peoples was across the Sahara, and after the spread of Islam across North Africa these caravan routes were in Muslim hands. Christians were forbidden to go beyond the Mediterranean port cities.

Even after Africa was circumnavigated by the Portuguese there was little or no access to the interior. The Dutch settled along the coast of South Africa, and there were Portuguese settlements on the west coast and in Portuguese East Africa. The Europeans, however, were generally confined to the coastal areas. For the most part the west coast area was not settled at all; it was merely the port of call for slave trading companies some of which kept "factors," or representatives there who bought the slaves brought from farther inland by Africans themselves.

Actually, entry into the continent of Africa except by air is extremely difficult even today. There are no rivers navigable from the coast into the interior. Cataracts in the Nile, swamps along the Niger, rapids in the Congo, and falls in the Zambezi block free entrance and exit. Nor are there any really good harbors along either the eastern or the western coasts. Added to these handicaps are deserts, tropical rain forests, predatory animals, and a host of insects and parasites to make life difficult. Malaria is endemic over wide areas of the continent and large areas of Central Africa are ravaged by tsetse flies which cause sleeping sickness and prevent keeping of domestic animals. In South and East Africa are found cattle keeping tribes but throughout much of Central and West Africa men have had to wrest their living from the soil without the aid of domestic animals to provide food, fertilizer, or power.

In spite of these handicaps many of the African peoples developed complex and sophisticated cultures. In the Sudanic area there were great Negro empires, and at a time when many North Europeans were just emerging from semibarbarism there flourished at Timbuktu a Negro-Arabic University that was famed throughout North Africa, Spain, and the Near East. Farther to the south were the Negro kingdoms of Ashanti, Dahomey, and Benin. These peoples were nonliterate, but they had developed elaborate social and political organizations, and there were among them skilled artists and craftsmen.

The development of the West Africans, like that of the American Indians, was interrupted from without. When the Moors were expelled from Spain, and civilization, not now in Muslim but in Christian hands, pushed westward across the Atlantic, Africa was left off the line of march, and her kingdoms were shut off from the expanding Western world. At about the same time Europeans began raiding the continent to get laborers for their colonies in the New World. For three hundred years a large portion of Africa was raped and plundered, her native kingdoms disorganized, her rulers and people demoralized, industry smothered or distorted. Moreover, the slave trade had hardly ended when the European nations began partitioning the continent among themselves without regard to natural, cultural, or linguistic boundaries. Only within the past decades have Africans begun to regain mastery in their own house.

Just as Northern and Western Europeans were long on the margins of the civilized world, living the lives of backwoodsmen, so today we find that there are many peoples who have been left off the line of march or who for other reasons have been, and may still be, at a disadvantage. The peoples in the islands that make up parts of Malaysia, Melanesia, Polynesia, and Micronesia were generally isolated, and for the most part they lacked both natural resources and the stimulation of contact. Some of the Polynesian peoples developed fairly sophisticated cultures, but most of the islands are tropical and many of them are small. In no area of the Pacific, including Australia, were there any large animals suitable for domestication, and many of the native plants available were of limited nutritional value. Hawaii, New Zealand, and Australia are now, of course, predominantly European in culture and to a large extent in population, and the Philippines, Malaya, and Indonesia are modern states though with many peoples that still follow traditional ways. Most of the other islands are still on the fringes of the modern world.

The conclusions from this look backward and around us seem obvious. No race or nation can claim to be made up of superior people. No people has remained in the lead throughout history. Our own British and North European forebears were "just natives" during a far longer period than they have been in places of leadership or than the United States has been a nation. Moreover, when the United States came into its own it had the whole of the civilized world's cultural contribution at its disposal, and it had one of the richest, most healthful, and most spacious areas of the world in which to develop. For any European, and particularly for any American, to scorn the old civilizations to which we all owe so much is to deny the very foundations on which our own culture rests. To despise the peoples who occupy the isolated, poor, unproductive, unhealthful, or overcrowded areas of the world is to forget that our North European ancestors themselves were for thousands of years among the world's isolated and backward peoples. To suppose that we are destined to stay on the top of the heap merely because we now find ourselves there is to fail to read—or heed—the lessons of history.

More foolish still is to take personal credit for the culture into which we were fortunate enough to be born, or to imagine that we could have done equally well had our birthplace been in one of the crowded or isolated places of the world with limited resources available. Perhaps most foolish of all is to claim superiority because of the pigmentation of our skin, the texture of our hair, or the shape of our features. Not only have men and women of all races helped to make America, but persons of many races have been among the richest and poorest, the most civilized and the most savage at every period of history. Some blond, blue-eyed white men roamed the forests of North Europe as barbarians long after some yellow and black men had become scholars, artists, and statesmen. Today the color of a man's skin is no guarantee of the qualities of his mind and character, nor are his race and origin any criteria of the contribution he may make to the common good.

A health director . . . reported this week that a small mouse, which presumably had been watching television, attacked a little girl and her full grown cat.

. . . both mouse and cat survived, and the incident is recorded here as a reminder that things seem to be changing. The mice of the world are no longer doing what the cats say.

JAMES RESTON*

10. PEOPLES IN TRANSITION

1. Ways of Looking at the World

Anthropologists have long concentrated on the study of simple or small scale societies that are self-contained wholes. Although information about such societies is necessary to building a body of knowledge about human behavior, the societies themselves are relatively unimportant as far as world affairs are concerned. Moreover, most of these societies are in process of change, and almost all of them are now parts of larger wholes. To understand the modern world these larger units must be taken into account.

Robert Redfield has suggested a way of roughly grouping societies in terms of their culture histories. There are the old civilizations, the peoples with a great tradition, some of which are still functioning as large scale societies even though their present world positions do not measure up to the proud roles they played in the past. The peoples in most of these still functioning primary civilizations, such as China, Korea, and India, are struggling to orient themselves to the modern technological world; some of them, notably in Japan, have achieved technological competence. In many places of the world, however, the present-day inhabitants are the physical and spatial descendants of greatness without being its cultural heirs. These are the peoples who live on in the great river valleys or in the midst of ancient ruins from which the glory has

* *The New York Times*, July 7, 1957.

long since departed, sometimes even from the memory of the peoples whose ancestors created it.

In other areas there are what have been called secondary civilizations, local cultures that have been more or less submerged under expanding and colonizing powers from elsewhere. In some areas the local cultures were largely destroyed, supplanted, or isolated as in America north of Mexico, in New Zealand, and Australia. In other areas, local cultures were overlaid and dominated by the invaders without being wholly destroyed in the process. Much of Latin America and many of the areas into which Hinduism and Islam spread fall into this category.

Wherever there is a great tradition there are also to be found little traditions; nowhere outside the simple, small scale society, and sometimes not even there, is there a single way of life. The literate, the wealthy, the sophisticated, the scholar, the priest, and the philosopher have a way of thought and a way of life that differs from that of the illiterate and unsophisticated masses. Moreover, the whole world is now, and for some decades has been, in a kind of revolutionary ferment that breaks down the barriers separating one kind of society and one kind of people from another. Ideas are being scattered to remote places as if they were seeds borne on the wind.

Another way of looking at the world is in terms of realized potential, and this view has led to the classification of countries into developed and underdeveloped groups. In *The Nature of the Non-Western World* Vera Micheles Dean makes the division between Western and non-Western countries. This dichotomy does not mean that the Western world is all of a piece or that being non-Western makes other peoples all alike. And, of course, Western in this sense is a state of mind, or a state of technological development, rather than a geographical position.

In the sense of high technological development, the Western world is primarily the world of Northern and Western Europe and the countries settled by peoples from this area. It is, as we have seen, a world developed during the past five hundred years. Southern and Eastern Europe went somewhat separate ways that left them apart from the main line of development, of what we now think of as modern Western civilization, and many of these countries would fall into a semi-Western or intermediate category.

The intermediate and highly developed countries are now in control of world affairs, but the fact that two-thirds of the world's peoples are in underdeveloped countries gives to them a potential influence of enormous magnitude. Furthermore, as we look at the characteristics of this great segment of mankind, we begin to understand the gap that separates them from the peoples who have greater economic advantages. For the most part, the underdeveloped world is desperately poor by Western standards; much of it is chronically hungry; it is weighted down with the burdens of poor health, poor sanitation, and inadequate medical care. It has a high rate of illiteracy, a generally low educational level, and it is technologically poor. In many of the underdeveloped countries there is a small, wealthy, upper class, but the privileges of this group are not generally shared by the masses. A middle class is often small or nonexistent.

Although there are wide differences between the old civilizations of Asia and the nonliterate cultures of Oceania and Africa these various non-Western peoples have many things in common besides those factors that place them in the underdeveloped category. Perhaps the two things that do most to give them a sense of unity can be summed up as colonialism and color.

We now know that an individual's pigmentation is not an important factor in his behavior. But since the majority of non-Western peoples are dark, and they live in the less favored areas of the world, it is not surprising that many Westerners consider color a symbol of backwardness and inferiority. And because, at one time or another, most of the non-Western peoples have been the victims of Western discrimination based on color, it is not surprising that many of them consider white skin a symbol of arrogance and an object of hatred.

Colonialism, too, is heavily weighted with racial connotations. During the period of exploration and conquest most of the non-Western world came under the control of European governments; even the countries that remained politically independent were subject to varying degrees of economic control. Many of the subject peoples reeled under the blow of too sudden, too violent, or too prolonged impact and were either annihilated or absorbed. What is now the United States, Canada, Australia, and New Zealand were taken from the hands of aboriginal populations. The majority of the Latin American countries have been, in varying degrees, colonized and Europeanized. In some of them, such as Argentina and Cuba, there are no aboriginals left. In others, the Indians still form a high proportion of the population; and in still others, the population represents varying degrees of mixture of Europeans, aboriginal Indians, and Negro peoples imported from Africa during the period of the slave trade.

In some areas, such as Southeast Asia, there have been successive waves of peoples and of cultural influences—Hindu, Buddhist, and Muslim peoples swept over large areas of the world long before modern Christian missionaries began their work or European governments started their colonial expansion. Ultimately, however, European governments gained political control of almost the whole of Africa, India, Southeast Asia, and the Pacific Islands, and maintained spheres of influence in East Asia and elsewhere.

No one needs to be told that the underdeveloped or non-Western world is now on the move. The day of Kipling's "silent, sullen peoples" has long since passed. Today, they are vocal and rebellious. One by one they are throwing off the control of the Western powers and the voice of their discontent can be heard around the world. The reasons for this revolution are fairly obvious though they are complex. When the European governments gained control they instituted programs of one kind and another that profoundly influenced existing cultures. Traders carried Western wares and Christian missionaries set up hospitals and schools as well as churches. In many parts of Africa and in some other areas the only schools existing until relatively recent years were those set up by the missions.

World War I marked the beginning of mobility and communication on a wide scale. During and since that time men from all over the world have fought in British, French, German, Dutch, Italian, and American armies on various fronts. During the Korean War men of various races, languages, and religions fought side by side in the same units, shared the same rations, and wore the same uniforms. They went back to their homes with new ideas, new standards, new values, and new desires. In the meantime, motion pictures, radios, television, and the printed page carried ideas and propaganda from one side of the world to another. Hordes of tourists swarmed over the globe. Government missions and agencies multiplied. Various commissions of the United Nations, international, state, and private agencies moved into troubled or needy areas. Thousands of students from all over the world began to study in the colleges and universities of the West, and foreign visitors in Europe and America became commonplace.

Something of the strength of this impact may be measured in its political manifestations. World War II saw the beginning of the end of European power in Asia and Africa. Today the list of recently independent countries is an impressive one: India, Pakistan, Ceylon, Burma, Malaya, the Republic of Indonesia, Israel, the Philippines, Libya, Tunisia, Morocco, the Sudan, and Ghana are among the nations that were not on the map as independent states until after the close of World War II. By the early 1960's another dozen or more independent states had been carved out of former European colonies in Africa.

To the free world an ominous factor in this changing situation is the fact that while most of the peoples formerly controlled by the old colonial powers have gained their independence, other peoples formerly independent have either been absorbed into the Soviet Union or have become puppet satellites of the Communist powers. Latvia, Estonia, and Lithuania are no longer independent entities. Tibet has lost whatever freedom it once possessed, and Korea, Vietnam, and Germany are divided. The constant stream of refugees who use any means to escape Communist-controlled countries is as significant as are the struggles of the newly independent nations to gain political stability and economic sufficiency.

The rejection of Western political control does not mean a rejection of Western civilization, particularly its material aspects. A part of the problem of these peoples on the move lies in the fact that many of them are trying to achieve within a period of a few years technological levels, social controls, and forms of government that it has taken the West generations to master. Many of the underdeveloped countries lack economic resources, an educated electorate, traditions of democracy, and experience in self-government. In some cases they have been catapulted from the Stone Age to the Nuclear Age in one generation. Failure to make this transition successfully is no evidence of their lack of capacity for self-government; it would be something of a miracle if people could wholly achieve such drastic changes in so brief a time. It is to our interest as well as to theirs that they make the transition as successfully and as quickly as possible, and with a minimum loss of their distinctive characteristics and treasured values.

2. Are Values Relative?

As the world becomes increasingly interdependent and as new nations become involved in international affairs cultural relativism becomes a matter of world concern. The study of other cultures indicates that almost any specific act, considered right and proper in one society, may be considered wrong in another society. Furthermore, judgments are based on experience, and each experience is interpreted in terms of one's own enculturation so that even our perception of the physical world is to some extent viewed through this enculturative screen.

Out of their experience with many cultures anthropologists see the importance of recognizing not only that peoples define things differently but that no item of culture can be fairly considered outside its cultural context. Cultures are wholes, and the values of any culture constitute a system in which each part takes its meaning from its relation to other parts. Any item of behavior therefore rests on certain basic premises, and its meaning is relative to these premises and to other associated behaviors. On this basis it is possible to conclude that while there are certain universals, or kinds of values, found in all cultures, there are no absolutes which apply equally to all societies, and all values are therefore relative to time, place, and circumstance. It would seem to follow then that each people should be allowed to observe its own patterns regardless of how they may look to other peoples with different patterns.

Even when allowing for the gross oversimplification of the statements just made a number of practical problems are immediately apparent. For one thing, what is a "society" or a "culture"? The question may be fairly simple when some small, isolated group of people is involved, but such isolated societies are now rare. For other peoples the question may be exceedingly complex, as was apparent following World War I when the principle of the "self-determination of peoples" was proposed. How small is the unit to be considered and what of the large number of geographic areas occupied by several peoples whose patterns are quite different? And what of minorities? What happens to the majority when the numerical minority is the educated, economically superior, ruling group? In dozens of areas of the world today there can be found current versions of these problems that confronted the League of Nations.

Many of the states that have come into being since World War I were artificially created political entities; few of them represent actual cultural unity, much less uniformity. For example, the Republic of the Congo has boundaries that were drawn years ago by Europeans without regard to tribal or even broader linguistic lines.

Within this area are numerous tribes speaking different languages. Some of these tribal groups are intermingled in the same territory, and many of them are traditional rivals if not enemies. What, then, is "Congo" culture?

Within some areas of Africa there are territories occupied by native-born Africans and also by native-born white persons of European ancestry, some of whose families have been in the region for hundreds of years. In some cases each group claims the right of "self-determination." The white person whose home in a given area was occupied by his ancestors through several generations cannot very well "go back" to some other part of the world. Whose culture is "the" culture of the area?

Similar problems are common in other areas. The Indian-Pakistani dispute over Kashmir is rooted in part in the fact that Kashmir had a predominantly Muslim population with a Hindu ruler. The partition of the old India into the modern states of India and Pakistan was itself a result of the fears and conflicts growing out of joint tenancy of a land by peoples who were divided by religious, linguistic, and cultural differences. Even the division of India into states has engendered bitter quarrels along linguistic lines. In Malaya, the conflict of interest between the Malay population and the long-resident Chinese involves not only race and national origin but religion, language, economic patterns, and cultural aspirations.

Another facet in the problem of cultural differences lies in the fact that in all societies, however defined, there are discrepancies between what most people actually do and what they say and believe one should do. There are also differences in the way people of different statuses perceive their own culture. No individual is ever familiar with the total content of the culture in which he participates; even in very simple societies there are certain things with which men are familiar and other things which only women know. As societies grow more complex, more stratified, or spread over broader territories, less and less of the total culture can be known by any one individual.

Two common practices further complicate cultural evaluations. On the one hand, most of us tend to compare our own ideal culture with other people's actual culture. Many Americans think of the United States as a Christian, democratic nation (our ideal culture), and they are shocked when other peoples point to various aspects of our life that are clearly neither Christian nor democratic. Students from other countries usually see clearly the seamy side of our real culture while they often stoutly defend their own ideal culture as being the way things really are back home.

The other common practice is to make judgments about whole countries and to ignore the differences between urban and rural peoples, between rich and poor, between upper and lower classes, or between culturally different ethnic groups. This practice is often extended to a whole continent and one who has been anywhere in Africa may be asked how "the Africans" dress or live or what their religion is. Peoples from other parts of the world often make the same sweeping judgments about the United States and for all of Latin America.

On the popular level today there are a variety of beliefs about relative values. On the one hand, there are those who think we should try to save the world by making other peoples over in our own image. Other persons take the extreme relativistic position that other peoples' ways are good for them, so we should live and let live. This latter position not only leaves us with all the problems of who the "other people" are, but also with the problems that arise when some of these "others" do not follow the let-live part of the rule. Not only may weaker peoples be taken over by the militarily stronger ones, but there is also the Communist model of imperialism, which operates by infiltration and subversion as well as by military force.

If the concept of cultural relativity is taken to mean that all culture patterns are equally "good" and that "one culture is as good as another," there can be little useful meaning in the idea. Even less tenable is the notion that because some pattern of behavior "works" in one culture it could profitably be transferred bodily somewhere else. The more useful set of concepts is that practices and beliefs must always be evaluated within the cultural context in which they occur, that cultures must be considered as wholes, and that the ways of any people are entitled to respect so long as they do not do violence to others.

In any community, the rights of any individual must take into account the rights of other individuals and the welfare of the total group. So in an increasingly interdependent world must the rights of groups, whether culturally or politically defined, take into account the rights of neighboring groups and of the world as a whole. There is no easy or simple answer as to how the rights of each group in a multicultured nation may be guarded, or how the rights of the small and weak may be protected from the encroachments of the powerful and strong, whether within a given society or nation or between societies and nations. And there is as yet no answer as to how the conflicting interests and ambitions of the major nations may be resolved. How peoples of diverse races, cultures, languages, religions, ideologies, and political loyalties can share an ever-shrinking planet has become the major unsolved problem confronting the human race in the twentieth century.

3. What Do They Want?

It is reported that the Balinese term for the time before the coming of the white man is "when the world was steady." Today it would be hard to find any place in which the world is still "steady." Everywhere people are on the move—slowly in some places, rapidly in others, explosively in still others. Such rapid change adds enormously to the difficulty of understanding other cultures or, indeed, of understanding one's own, for the change is rarely uniform or complete. In our own society there are persons who buy the latest model cars, whose houses are filled with the most modern comforts and conveniences, whose physical health and perhaps life itself may have been preserved by the latest medical discoveries, but who are firmly opposed to any sort of social change. They are quite willing to live physically in the jet age, but they wish to preserve the patterns of their grandfathers, if not those of Washington and Jefferson, as far as relations between races, classes, and nations are concerned.

By the same token, people in the underdeveloped societies may be ready to accept machinery as something useful and desirable, but may display no corresponding interest in developing the patterns, habits, and skills necessary to the care and effective use of such machinery. The people may want the things which Westerners have but be quite unwilling to accept the discipline of regular work habits essential to the achievement of an economic level that would make such things possible. In other cultures, as sometimes in our own, the easy way may be more appealing than a way that is new or strange, or that calls for increased effort. Sometimes there are vested interests involved, or there may be a centuries-old heritage of suspicion, fear, and distrust of anything new. Sometimes there are treasured values that appear to be threatened by the new ways.

From missionaries and representatives of other agencies seeking to help the people of underdeveloped countries come countless

stories of baffled and bewildered Westerners who have found themselves up against a seemingly senseless blank wall of indifference or
resistance. There may be simply a stubborn refusal to consider a
new program, or there may be a total lack of understanding of the
relation between sanitation and health, or a refusal to believe that
so small a creature as a fly or a mosquito—much less a germ that
cannot be seen—could possibly cause disease.

There are other places in which the people are militantly demanding a chance at the new ways though they may not always comprehend the price of progress. The people who call loudest for
freedom and independence may not have the remotest conception of
the responsibilities involved in either of them. People who have had
no experience in self-government have sometimes welcomed the
empty promises of totalitarianism only to discover too late that they
had traded a lesser for a greater bondage. Even when the individual
welcomes new ways he may find himself caught in the clutches of a
family system or tribal rules that nullify any advantage he might
otherwise enjoy.

People in other cultures often have difficulty in comprehending
the totality of the Western ways they would adopt. There have been
serious social consequences when Western standards and patterns
were imposed on local cultures in the absence of an understanding
of local practices on the part of the Westerner and with no comprehension of the Western standards by the native people. Sometimes,
in fact, the Westerners have indirectly encouraged the very practices
they hoped to eradicate. Sometimes they have been responsible for
substituting a greater for a lesser evil as when the premature elimination of polygamy has resulted in an increase in prostitution.

One of the recurring problems of acculturation grows out of the
fact that in many non-Western societies people recognize responsibility only where personal relations are involved. Many Westerners
have been shocked at the seeming callousness of other peoples with
regard to the human suffering around them. But these same people
might impoverish themselves to provide for their relatives or their
distant clansmen. The American's impersonal giving to causes and
to peoples of whom he has no personal knowledge or connection
may arouse as much suspicion as gratitude. It is such differences in
concepts that account for many instances of people's accepting food
packages or other gifts not with thanks but with the response, "You
are indeed our relative."

Such concepts have often proved a baffling obstacle to relief

efforts, to the operation of social services, and even to the establishment of representative government. Missionaries attempting to train
nurses and medical assistants in central Africa have found great
difficulty in getting across the idea that all patients in the hospital
were entitled to care and attention in proportion to their needs. The
native helpers felt they should favor the patients from their own
tribes to the neglect of outsiders. In many other societies the man
who is given a job thinks first of looking after the interests of his
relatives. Within their system of values duty to one's own kin is
supposed to take precedence over any other obligation, and the head
of a school or government official who did not put his relatives into
jobs, regardless of their qualifications, would be severely criticized
not only by his family but by the community as a whole.

Such cultural definitions may extend to honesty, truthfulness, and
loyalty. There are many societies in which it is expected that one
should be truthful and honest in dealings with one's own people but
honesty, truthfulness, and loyalty as abstract virtues may not be a
part of the value system. In some cultures, the deception or defraud-
ing of outsiders may be considered a virtue if it enables one to take
better care of those to whom he owes loyalty and support. Where
honesty and truthfulness are functions of personal relationships,
they are not accorded to persons who do not fall within the circle
of one's loyalties.

The Westerner is often puzzled and disillusioned at what to him
seems to be a distorted sense of values on the part of an African,
Asian, or Latin American villager who spends money on some unnecessary gadget when he and his family lack the most elementary
necessities. The commonest of these minor status symbols appear to
be the fountain pen, the watch, and the bicycle; more recently the
radio, sunglasses, a camera, or a walking cane. But such gadgets—
even when bought by persons who cannot use them—are no sillier
than some of our own status symbols such as fins and chrome on
cars, and picture windows where there is no view. A literate society
in which numerous families own boats and swimming pools but no
books might appear odd to some other peoples. The pen, the watch,
and the bicycle, on the other hand, may represent not only worthy
aspirations but a platform from which to reach for the next level.
The bicycle, although it serves as a status symbol, is also a practical
means of locomotion. The pen is a symbol of literacy and can be as
important to the barely literate as the "failed B.A." once was in a

society in which getting to college at all was an achievement to boast of. Whether one can tell time or not, a watch is a symbolic recognition of a world in which time is important and precisely recorded.

One of the factors in the problem of transition is the growing sense of deprivation felt by people who are becoming aware of the possibilities of more and better food and clothing, medical care, education, and other "good things" once undreamed of. As these things become possibilities, what was once simply their absence becomes a deeply felt deprivation, with consequent unhappiness and frustration. In *The Death of Africa*, Peter Ritner suggests that in an African village where everybody wore skins or grass fiber a man who owned a pair of pants felt rich. But when he goes to a community where everybody wears pants he is not contented because a pair of pants no longer represents riches but the minimum level of what one can get along with. If a man's concept of what constitutes the minimum level rises faster than his actual level, his discontent grows though he may actually have more than he did before. One of the acute problems in underdeveloped countries grows out of the fact that contact with Westerners who have so much raises the non-Westerner's level of aspiration and expectation faster than such aspirations and expectations can be realized. The result is discontent and frustration.

As the underdeveloped countries advance economically, the gap between the more privileged and the less fortunate becomes less tolerable to the latter. In many of these underdeveloped areas there have always been the very rich and the very poor, but they lived in different worlds. In an earlier day the most that the poor dreamed of asking was that the rich be generous and kind. This was what the slave hoped of his master, and the servant expected no more and hoped for no less from his European employer. Kindness and generosity are no longer enough, and growing numbers of people aspire to other than menial jobs devoted to making more fortunate people comfortable.

Today, the peoples of the world are in the midst of what has been called a revolution of rising expectations. They are demanding all kinds of things that might be summed up as a chance for the good life. To be sure, the peoples of the world would not all agree on the details of what constitutes the good life, but everywhere they are beginning to ask for freedom from constant hunger, from disease, from premature death, from grinding poverty, and from endless toil. Increasingly they are asking for land reform, medical care, schools, roads, and a voice in their own affairs.

If we read aright the signs of recent years we will know that economic development alone is not enough. The non-Western peoples are asking freedom from fear and oppression, and perhaps most of all they want freedom from contempt and the stigma of inferiority. Increasingly they are demanding that they be freed, at any cost, from any form of domination by the West. Sometimes their wants are contradictory: they cling to old customs that are incompatible with their new desires. They do not always want democracy as we understand it, and they do not always know how to handle freedom when it is achieved. Their newly formed governments may sometimes be corrupt and dictatorial and their economic disadvantage may sometimes grow greater rather than less. But none of them has yet asked for a return of colonial government. The one thing the peoples of the non-Western world seem to be unanimous about is that they wish to be allowed to make their own mistakes in their own way.

4. America and the World

Since the beginning of World War I, mankind has been in the throes of a world revolution, the shape of which is now becoming discernible. One of the major characteristics of this revolution is the virtual annihilation of distance with a corresponding increase in the speed of intercommunication and a concomitant increase in man's interdependence. This means, of course, that there are no longer any real physical barriers separating one people from another. There are still language barriers, so far as person-to-person communication is concerned, but simultaneous translations and space-located telephone and television relay stations are opening up new levels of contact, and our former spatial relationships have largely lost their meaning.

Another new element in the modern world is, of course, the vast power of destruction that man has at his disposal. In earlier times wars could and did have bitter consequences, but they did not cause total destruction even in limited areas. Today nations have the power to destroy one another—and that power is gradually finding its way into more and more hands. Moreover, there looms on the horizon the certainty that man could render the earth itself un-inhabitable.

The final and most portentous factor in our new situation is that for the first time in man's history the entire globe is involved at once. In earlier times nation after nation came to power, only to fall behind and be supplanted by another; but civilization itself did not perish because there were always other peoples left to carry on. Today, our progress in technology, our increase in rapid communication, our economic interdependence, and the enormous power at man's disposal, have tied us all together and made each of us hostages to the others' fortunes. Whether we like it or not, for good or ill, and in a way John Donne could not have dreamed of, we are now involved in mankind.

We have heard a great deal in recent years about one world, world government, and a world culture. It is important that we be clear about the differences in these three ideas. We now live in one world in the sense that we have become globally interrelated and interdependent; the facts have become planetary. World government implies some kind of formal organization with more centralized control than would now seem practicable. In view of the diversity of the present governments in the world, the United Nations represents a long step toward world order and if it can be the means of preventing a global holocaust we shall be fortunate. A world culture in the sense of any appreciable degree of uniformity in cultural patterns would—even if it were possible—represent a tremendous loss and little if any gain. Cultural likeness has never kept peoples from going to war against one another, and cultural uniformity would be no guarantee of peace. It does not matter how culturally diverse we are so long as we agree on certain basic values, one of which must be respect for one another's cultural differences. Our problem is how to live together, not how to become alike.

The answer to this basic problem of how we may turn man's energies away from world destruction to peace and cooperation for the common good lies in another new aspect of human history. For the first time in man's history we could solve the problem of sharing the planet in peace if we chose to do so and were willing to direct our full energies to that end. The new thing is not that we now know enough to solve our problems because the simple truth is that we do not know enough. What is new is that we now know how to go about getting the knowledge that we need.

The whole globe is known to us. All the records of man's accumulated knowledge could be assembled. We can communicate with one another across the world in a matter of moments and there are no longer insuperable language barriers. We know what cultural differences mean and something of how cultures function. We know that cultural behavior is learned and that it can be modified. We know how national loyalties are developed and why men feel as they do about their own ways. We know that racial differences are of no real consequence in human behavior unless we make them so. We know that all normal human beings can learn and can be taught. We know how further knowledge of human behavior can be acquired and how the skills necessary to meet human needs can be developed. And we really know, too, that the basic problem confronting the world is how men can live with themselves and their fellow men.

We know all these things, and yet we continue to act as if they were not true. The gap between our knowledge of the physical world and our understanding of human behavior and human society is wide and deep. For generations Western man has devoted his thought, his energies, and his resources to the conquest of the physical world. In recent decades billions of dollars in private and public funds and billions of man hours directed by our best minds have gone into the research laboratories and the plants out of which have come the streams of products that constitute the modern miracles of our age. But there has been no even remotely comparable effort to increase our understanding and our skill in the fields of human behavior, human relations, and international understanding.

We recognize the complexity of the human organism by continuous medical research and by requiring specialized training for the medical profession. We have begun, belatedly, to recognize that we need specialists who know not only anatomy and physiology but also about man's mental and emotional behavior. For the most part, however, we seem to be almost completely lacking in awareness that group behavior can be studied and perhaps, in time, predicted and controlled. The study of social structure, social process, and problems of social, political, and international relations are to most people subjects of no practical consequence. Our expenditures for research in these areas are absurdly small.

Yet our own society is plagued with problems of poverty in the midst of plenty, unemployment, racial and religious prejudice, graft, corruption, crime, and juvenile delinquency. In our relations with the rest of the world we are in a constant state of cold war or threats of global war. We have given away millions of dollars to the rest of the world, but we know so little about human behavior and the values of other cultures that our gifts often make enemies rather than friends. The individual who goes out to help the people of another culture without at least some elementary understanding of what culture is and how it operates is in the class with the medically untrained person who attempts to treat the sick. At least some of the turmoil in various parts of the world might have been avoided if Western government officials, technicians, missionaries, and others who undertook to initiate or direct changes had known as much about culture, human society, and social change as the average physician knows about the anatomy and physiology of the human body.

To bridge the gap between our knowledge of the physical world and our understanding of human behavior will be a formidable task because we do not now have the necessary knowledge and skills. We only know how such knowledge and skills may be obtained. In a democracy such a program is possible only when enough individuals accept the support and implementation of it as their personal responsibility. To solve our problems of human relations calls for a drastic revision of our values as measured by the things to which we devote our time, our energies, and our funds.

Moreover, if we do find any reasonably satisfactory solutions we must accept the fact that they will not be permanent ones. Man's progress is recorded, not in his germ plasm, but in his social institutions—and these institutions must be eternally watched over, guarded, reinforced, and at times revised and altered as conditions change. Being informed about the world we live in and meeting our responsibilities of citizenship are not chores that can be tossed off in a few hours once or twice a year. They belong rather in a category of daily necessities of living like eating and sleeping, taking a bath, and brushing one's teeth. Only by accepting the responsibility of citizenship and the daily duties it implies can we have much hope of creating a world in which men can live at peace or, for that matter, live at all.

Solutions to our problems will not come through pious hopes and wishful thinking, nor through any sort of magic formula. If we find workable answers we shall find them in the same way that we have found solutions to the problems of the physical world, that is, by using our minds and our energies to bring them about. We do not know whether finding ways by which men can live together is a task more difficult than unlocking the secrets of the atom because we have never made efforts to find the former that even remotely approximate the efforts devoted to the latter. Until we are willing to make such efforts there is little hope of finding answers to the problems now besetting the world.

There are those who will say that no society can change its own value system. But here our very diversity is our strength, for there are millions of Americans who do value persons above things, who do cherish freedom and democratic values, and who are willing to subordinate personal interest to the common good. Moreover, we as a people are theoretically committed to such values however imperfectly we live up to them and even deny them by our behavior. One does not have to nurse "the illusion of omnipotence" to reject the theory that we are so entirely the creatures of our culture that we have no control at all over our own destiny.

Changing the behavior of our own society does not, of course, guarantee any change in other nations. But we may well remember that the underdeveloped world is a vast aggregate of almost two billion people most of whom have yet to choose the road they will follow. Whether they choose totalitarianism or freedom may well depend on the willingness of the American people to practice genuine democracy at home, and to behave with understanding, wisdom, and consistency in our relations with the rest of the world.

NOTES AND
REFERENCES

This section and the Bibliography together are designed to identify and give credit to some of the numerous sources used in the preparation of this book, and to give some guidance to those wishing to do further reading in general or specific areas.

References are identified only by author and date. The full reference to authors mentioned here or in the text may be found in the Bibliography, which is divided into three main categories: I. Standard General Textbooks; II. General References and Sources; III. Area and Tribal Studies. The Area and Tribal Studies are further divided into Area Background Studies and Monographs on Tribal Groups. The latter is further subdivided into geographical areas. Within each category or subcategory books are listed alphabetically by author.

The tribal peoples are grouped into the general areas of Africa, the Americas (Indians and Eskimo), India (aboriginal or village groups), and the Pacific. Within the Pacific area peoples are generally grouped into Malaysia (the Philippines, the Malay Peninsula, and the islands extending from the Malay Peninsula to, but not including, New Guinea); Melanesia (the football-shaped area from New Guinea to Fiji); Polynesia (the islands within the triangle formed by Hawaii, New Zealand, and Easter Island); and Micronesia (the small islands roughly north of Melanesia). Included in this area also are the Andaman Islands and the aboriginal tribes of Australia. The Pacific islands are sometimes referred to collectively as Oceania. The exact location of the various peoples mentioned will be found in Spencer and Johnson (1960).

To save the reader the burden of too many strange names an effort was made to limit specific illustrations to a few tribes, such as the Eskimo, and the Navaho, Hopi, and Crow among American Indians; the Ashanti, Dahomeans, Nuer, Chaga, Zulu, Thonga, and Nyakyusa of Africa; the Hos of India; the Kalingas of the Philippines; the Kwoma, Trobrianders, and Dobuans of Melanesia; the Tikopia and Ontong Javanese of Polynesia; the Andaman Islanders, and the Arunta of Australia. The monographs listed in the Bibliography are the ones most heavily drawn on in preparing this volume. Many others that were used in one way or another are omitted for want of space.

1. MAN AND CULTURE

Further elaboration of most of the topics treated in this chapter will be found in any of the books listed under Standard General Textbooks.

Other books of special interest to the general reader are Benedict (1946), Evans-Pritchard (1952, 1954), Goldschmidt (1960), Kluckhohn (1949), Lee (1959), and Linton (1955).

For language, see any of the standard textbooks, or Hayakawa (1939) or Hoijer (1954).

Most of the standard texts give classifications of races. For further discussion of race see Bates (1961), Firth (1938), Howells (1959), La Barre (1954), or Krogman in Linton (1945). A very simple but useful presentation will be found in Boyd and Asimov (1955). For a summary statement on race differences see Brown in Clift, Anderson, and Hullfish (1962). See also Garn (1961).

Books of readings on various subjects and different cultures are Coon (1948), Forde (1934), Fried (1959), Goldschmidt (1960), Hoebel, Jennings, and Smith (1955), and Service (1958).

For the New Guinea tribe mentioned see Whiting (1941) and for the Africans, Evans-Pritchard (1940, 1956).

For the specific tribes mentioned in the text see the Monographs on Tribal Groups in the Bibliography.

2. THE WORK OF THE WORLD

Most of the standard textbooks listed will give further elaboration of the material discussed in this Chapter. Books dealing specifically with economics or technology are Forde (1934) Herskovits (1952), and Richards (1939).

All of the monographs dealing with specific tribes discuss the handling of the problems of food, clothing, and shelter, the instrumental means used, and the division of labor. For a general discussion of the sex division of labor see Mead (1935, 1949).

3. HOW PEOPLE LIVE TOGETHER

Treatment of the various systems of kinship and marriage will be found in any of the standard textbooks. Most of the general books on ethnology or social anthropology discuss kinship patterns. See particularly Lowie (1948), and Murdock (1949).

All of the tribal monographs give details of the kinship system. For the details of a number of American Indian tribes see Eggan (1955); for African tribes, see Radcliffe-Brown and Forde (1950).

The instance of the Chinese man who married two women to fulfill his obligations as a son and as an adopted son was reported in a personal communication. For a similar instance see Opler (1959).

For the specific tribes mentioned in the text see the Monographs on Tribal Groups in the Bibliography.

4. FROM BIRTH TO DEATH

Most of the standard textbooks discuss the life cycle, and nearly all monographs give the details for the particular culture. For general treatment of the socialization process see Davis (1948), Mead (1949), Mead and Wolfenstein (1955), Montagu (1955), Pettit (1946), and Whiting and Child (1953).

Other groups whose socialization patterns are treated at length in the monographs are the Manus, Mead (1930), the Samoans, Mead (1928), the Kwoma, Whiting (1941), the Hopi, Dennis (1940), the Navaho, Leighton and Kluckhohn (1947), and the Ngoni, Read (1960).

For other tribes specifically referred to in the text see the Monographs on Tribal Groups in the Bibliography.

5. THE EMBROIDERY OF LIFE

Basic textbooks in anthropology vary in the amount of attention given to the arts. Good general sources are Boas (1938), Linton (1955), and Lowie (1940). For art, particularly that of American Indians, see Boas (1955).

Monographs also vary in the amount of attention given to this aspect of culture. Good treatment will be found in Rattray (1927) for the Ashanti, and Herskovits (1938) for the Dahomeans.

For the tribes specifically mentioned in the text see the Monographs on Tribal Groups in the Bibliography.

6. HOW DO THEY DEFINE IT?

All of the standard texts and most of the general books in anthropology deal in one way or another with cultural definitions. Particularly useful are Lee (1959), Hall (1959), Hallowell (1955), Hsu (1953), Kaplan (1961), Opler (1956, 1959), Kluckhohn (1949), and any of the books by Redfield.

For culturally defined weeping see Radcliffe-Brown (1933). For culturally defined manifestation of neuroses see Hallowell (1955), Opler (1956, 1959), and Kaplan (1961).

For a discussion of "polite form" among American Indians see Eggan (1955). Various African peoples regard spitting as a ritual act; see Raum (1940) and Junod (1912). For differing attitudes toward human and animal wastes see Evans-Pritchard (1940), Schapera (1930) and Spencer (1959). For differing definitions of masculine and feminine behavior see Mead (1935, 1949), and Ford and Beach (1952).

For the tribes specifically mentioned in the text see the Monographs on Tribal Groups in the Bibliography.

7. THE SYSTEM OF VALUES

For a discussion of American values relative to those of other peoples see Hsu (1953), Lee (1959), Maraini (1959), Powdermaker (1950), and Warner (1953).

For values in various African societies see Forde (1954); for various American Indian groups see Eggan (1955).

For the problems of witchcraft and sorcery in Africa see Evans-Pritchard (1937) and Wilson (1951). Other good discussions of the subject will be found in Lessa and Vogt (1958).

For a discussion of positive and negative sanctions and the function of the patterns of avoidance and licensed familiarity see Radcliffe-Brown (1952) and Eggan (1955).

For the tribes mentioned in the text see the Monographs on Tribal Groups in the Bibliography.

8. RELIGION IN CULTURE

For a general discussion of religion as seen by anthropologists see Benedict in Boas (1938), Herskovits (1948), and Redfield (1956). Evans-Pritchard (1956) has a good discussion of the early theories on the origin of religion. One of the best general treatments will be found in Lessa and Vogt (1958).

For religion in simple societies see Lowie (1924), Goode (1951), Ferm (1950), Howells (1948), Malinowski (1948). Leslie (1960) has a good bibliography.

For the world religions see Jurji (1946).

For the peoples mentioned in the text see the Monograph on Tribal Groups in the Bibliography.

9. THE LONG ROAD

The standard texts particularly useful for this chapter are Boas (1938), Kroeber (1948), and Titiev (1959). Other useful books of particular interest to the general reader are Childe (1946, 1951), Coon (1954), Howells (1954), Linton (1955), and Montagu (1958).

For a brief discussion of the African background and the effect of the slave trade on African cultures see Brown (1957). For American Indians before Columbus see Martin, Quimby, and Collier (1947).

For a look at some of the underdeveloped areas of the world from various points of view see Dean (1957) and Rowan (1956). Linton (1949) is still useful. For other areas see the volumes listed under Area Background Studies in the Bibliography.

10. PEOPLES IN TRANSITION

Particularly useful for the opening sections of this chapter are Redfield (1953, 1956), Dean (1957), and Linton (1945, 1949).

For the problems involved in underdeveloped countries see also Mead (1953), Spicer (1952), Staley (1954), Ritner (1960), and the books listed under Area Background Studies in the Bibliography.

For an illuminating article on minor status symbols see C. Harley Gratton, "The Things the World Wants" in *Harper's*, November 1956.

For a discussion of cultural relativism see Herskovits (1948, 1955), Kluckhohn (1949), and Redfield (1953, 1955, 1956).

For the point of view of those who think that no society can change its value system, see White (1949, 1959).

SELECTED
BIBLIOGRAPHY

This Bibliography includes books mentioned but not completely identified in the text or in the *Notes and References*, the major sources used by the author, and books for further reading. For comments on books and suggestions for using the Bibliography, see *Notes and References*.

1. STANDARD GENERAL TEXTBOOKS

Beals, Ralph L. and Harry Hoijer, *An Introduction to Anthropology*, 2nd ed. New York: The Macmillan Company, 1959.

Boas, Franz and others, *General Anthropology*, Boston: D. C. Heath & Company, 1938.

Gillin, John, *The Ways of Men*, New York: Appleton-Century-Crofts, Inc., 1948.

Herskovits, Melville J., *Man and His Works*, New York: Alfred A. Knopf, Inc., 1948.

——, *Cultural Anthropology* (an abridged edition of *Man and His Works*), New York: Alfred A. Knopf, Inc., 1955.

Hoebel, E. Adamson, *Man in the Primitive World*, 2nd ed. New York: McGraw-Hill Book Co., Inc., 1958.

Honigmann, John J., *The World of Man*, New York: Harper & Row, Publishers, 1959.

Jacobs, Melville and Bernhard J. Stern, *General Anthropology*, New York: Barnes & Noble, Inc., 1958.

Keesing, Felix M., *Cultural Anthropology*, New York: Holt, Rinehart & Winston, Inc., 1958.

Kroeber, A. L., *Anthropology*, New York: Harcourt, Brace & World, Inc., 1948.

Linton, Ralph, *The Study of Man*, New York: Appleton-Century-Crofts, Inc., 1936.

Lowie, Robert H., *An Introduction to Cultural Anthropology*, New York: Farrar, Straus & Cudahy, Inc., 1940.

Piddington, Ralph, *An Introduction to Social Anthropology*, London: Oliver and Boyd, 1950, 2 vols.

Shapiro, Harry L., ed., *Man, Culture and Society*, New York: Oxford University Press, Inc., 1956.

Titiev, Mischa, *Introduction to Cultural Anthropology*, New York: Holt, Rinehart & Winston, Inc., 1959.

Turney-High, Harry Holbert, *General Anthropology,* New York: Thomas Y. Crowell Company, 1949.

2. GENERAL REFERENCES AND SOURCES

Bates, Marston, *Man in Nature,* Englewood Cliffs, N.J.: Prentice-Hall, Inc., 1961.

Benedict, Ruth, *Patterns of Culture,* New York: New American Library of World Literature, Inc., 1946.

Boas, Franz, *Primitive Art,* New York: Dover Publications, Inc., 1955.

Boyd, William C., *Genetics and the Races of Man,* Boston: Little, Brown & Co., 1950.

———, and Isaac Asimov, *Races and Peoples,* New York: Abelard-Schuman Ltd., 1955.

Brown, Ina Corinne, *The Story of the American Negro,* New York: Friendship Press, 1957.

Childe, Gordon, *What Happened in History,* New York: Penguin Books, Inc., 1946.

———, *Man Makes Himself,* New York: New American Library of World Literature, Inc., 1951.

Clift, Virgil A., Archibald W. Anderson, and H. Gordon Hullfish, eds., *Negro Education in America,* New York: Harper & Row, Publishers, 1962.

Coon, Carleton S., *The Story of Man,* New York: Alfred A. Knopf, Inc., 1954.

———, ed., *A Reader in General Anthropology,* New York: Holt, Rinehart & Winston, Inc., 1948.

Davis, Allison, *Social-Class Influences upon Learning,* Cambridge, Mass.: Harvard University Press, 1948.

Durkheim, Émile, *The Elementary Forms of the Religious Life.* Tr. G. Joseph Ward Swain, London: George Allen & Unwin, Ltd., 1915.

Eiseley, Loren, *The Firmament of Time,* New York: Atheneum Publishers, 1960.

Evans-Pritchard, E. E., *Social Anthropology,* Glencoe, Ill.: Free Press of Glencoe, Inc., 1952.

——— and others, *The Institutions of Primitive Society,* Glencoe, Ill.: Free Press of Glencoe, Inc., 1954.

Ferm, Virgilius, ed., *Forgotten Religions,* New York: Philosophical Library, Inc., 1950.

Firth, Raymond, *Human Types,* New York: Thomas Nelson & Sons, 1938.

Ford, Clellan S. and Frank A. Beach, *Patterns of Sexual Behavior,* New York: Harper & Row, Publishers, 1952.

Forde, C. Daryll, *Habitat, Economy and Society*, New York: E. P. Dutton & Co., Inc., 1934.

Frazer, James F., *The Golden Bough*, (one vol. ed.) New York: The Macmillan Company, 1930.

Freud, Sigmund, *Totem and Taboo*, translated by A. A. Brill, New York: Moffat, Yard & Co., 1918.

Fried, M. H., *Readings in Anthropology*, New York: Thomas Y. Crowell Company, 1959.

Garn, Stanley, *Human Races*, Springfield, Ill.: Charles C Thomas, Publisher, 1961.

Goldschmidt, Walter, *Exploring the Ways of Mankind*, New York: Holt, Rinehart & Winston, Inc., 1960.

Goode, William J., *Religion Among the Primitives*, Glencoe, Ill.: Free Press of Glencoe, Inc., 1951.

Grimble, Sir Arthur, *We Chose the Islands*, New York: William Morrow & Co., Inc., 1952.

Hall, Edward T., *The Silent Language*, Garden City, N.Y.: Doubleday & Company, Inc., 1959.

Hallowell, A. Irving, *Culture and Experience*, Philadelphia: University of Pennsylvania Press, 1955.

Hayakawa, S. I., *Language in Action*, New York: Harcourt, Brace & World, Inc., 1939.

Herodotus, *The History of Herodotus*, trans. by George Rawlinson, New York: Tudor Publishing Co., 1939.

Herskovits, Melville J., *Economic Anthropology*, New York: Alfred A. Knopf, Inc., 1952.

Hoebel, E. Adamson, Jesse D. Jennings and Elmer R. Smith, *Readings in Anthropology*, New York: McGraw-Hill Book Co., Inc., 1955.

Hoijer, Harry, ed., *Language in Culture*, Chicago: University of Chicago Press, 1954.

Howells, William, *Mankind in the Making*, Garden City, N.Y.: Doubleday & Company, Inc., 1959.

———, *Back of History*, Garden City, N.Y.: Doubleday & Company, Inc., 1954.

———, *The Heathens—Primitive Man and His Religions*, Garden City, N.Y.: Doubleday & Company, Inc., 1948.

Jurji, Edward J., ed., *The Great Religions of the Modern World*, Princeton, N.J.: Princeton University Press, 1946.

Kaplan, Bert, ed., *Studying Personality Cross-Culturally*, Evanston, Ill.: Row, Peterson & Company, 1961.

Kluckhohn, Clyde, *Mirror for Man*, New York: McGraw-Hill Book Co., Inc., 1949.

Kroeber, Alfred L., ed. *Anthropology Today. An Encyclopedic Inventory,* Chicago: University of Chicago Press, 1953.

La Barre, Weston, *The Human Animal,* Chicago: University of Chicago Press, 1954.

Lee, Dorothy, *Freedom and Culture,* Englewood Cliffs, N.J.: Prentice-Hall, Inc., 1959.

Lerner, Daniel, ed., *The Human Meaning of the Social Sciences,* New York: Meridian Books, 1959.

Leslie, Charles, *Anthropology of Folk Religion,* New York: Alfred A. Knopf, Inc., 1960.

Lessa, William A., and Evon Z. Vogt, *Reader in Comparative Religion. An Anthropological Approach,* Evanston, Ill.: Row, Peterson & Company, 1958.

Linton, Ralph, ed., *The Science of Man in the World Crisis,* New York: Columbia University Press, 1945.

———, *The Tree of Culture,* New York: Alfred A. Knopf, Inc., 1955.

Lowie, Robert, *Social Organization,* New York: Holt, Rinehart & Winston, Inc., 1948.

———, *Primitive Religion,* New York: Boni and Liveright, 1924.

Malinowski, Bronislaw, *Magic, Science and Religion,* Glencoe, Ill.: Free Press of Glencoe, Inc., 1948.

Mead, Margaret, *Sex and Temperament in Three Primitive Societies,* New York: William Morrow & Co., Inc., 1935.

———, *Male and Female,* New York: William Morrow & Co., Inc., 1949.

———, ed., *Cultural Patterns and Technical Change,* Paris: UNESCO, 1953.

——— and Martha Wolfenstein, eds., *Childhood in Contemporary Cultures,* Chicago: University of Chicago Press, 1955.

Melland, Frank, and Cullen Young, *African Dilemma,* London: The United Society for Christian Literature, 1937.

Montagu, Ashley, *Man: His First Million Years,* New York: New American Library of World Literature, Inc., 1958.

———, *The Direction of Human Development,* New York: Harper & Row, Publishers, 1955.

———, *Education and Human Relations,* New York: Grove Press, 1958.

Murdock, George Peter, *Social Structure,* New York: The Macmillan Company, 1949.

Opler, Marvin K., ed., *Culture and Mental Health,* New York: The Macmillan Company, 1959.

———, *Culture, Psychiatry and Human Values,* Springfield, Ill.: Charles C Thomas, Publisher, 1956.

Pettit, George A., *Primitive Education in North America,* Berkeley and Los Angeles: University of California Press, 1946.

Powdermaker, Hortense, *Hollywood, the Dream Factory*, Boston: Little, Brown & Co., 1950.

Radcliffe-Brown, A. R., *Structure and Function in Primitive Society*, Glencoe, Ill.: Free Press of Glencoe, Inc., 1952.

Redfield, Robert, *The Primitive World and Its Transformations*, Ithaca, N.Y.: Cornell University Press, 1953.

————, *Peasant Society and Culture*, Chicago: University of Chicago Press, 1956.

————, *The Little Community*, Chicago: University of Chicago Press, 1955.

Ritner, Peter, *The Death of Africa*, New York: The Macmillan Company, 1960.

Robinson, James Harvey, *The Mind in the Making*, New York: Harper & Row, Publishers, 1921.

Rowan, Carl T., *The Pitiful and the Proud*, New York: Random House, Inc., 1956.

Service, Elman R., *A Profile of Primitive Culture*, New York: Harper & Row, Publishers, 1958.

Smith, Edwin W., *African Ideas of God, a Symposium*, London: Edinburgh House Press, 1950.

Spencer, Robert F. and Elden Johnson, *Atlas for Anthropology*, Dubuque, Iowa: William C. Brown Company, Publishers, 1960.

Spicer, E. H., ed., *Human Problems in Technological Change*, New York: Russell Sage Foundation, 1952.

Sugimoto, Etsu Inagaki, *Daughter of the Samurai*, Garden City, N.Y.: Doubleday & Company, Inc., 1928.

Staley, Eugene, *The Future of Underdeveloped Countries*, New York: Harper & Row, Publishers, 1954.

Tax, Sol, and others, eds., *An Appraisal of Anthropology Today*, Chicago: University of Chicago Press, 1953.

Tylor, Edward B., *Primitive Culture*, New York: Holt, Rinehart & Winston, Inc., 1874, 2 vols.

Wallace, Anthony F. C., *Culture and Personality*, New York: Random House, Inc., 1961.

Warner, W. Lloyd, *American Life: Dream and Reality*, Chicago: University of Chicago Press, 1953.

White, Leslie A., *The Science of Culture*, New York: Farrar, Straus & Cudahy, Inc., 1949.

————, *The Evolution of Culture*, New York: McGraw-Hill Book Co., Inc., 1959.

Whiting, John W. M. and Irwin L. Child, *Child Training and Personality: A Cross-Cultural Study*, New Haven: Yale University Press, 1953.

3. AREA AND TRIBAL STUDIES

1. Area Background Studies

Adams, Richard N. and others, *Social Change in Latin America Today*, New York: Alfred A. Knopf, Inc., 1961.

Bailey, Helen Miller and A. P. Nasatir, *Latin America: The Development of Its Civilization*, Englewood Cliffs, N.J.: Prentice-Hall, Inc., 1960.

Cole, Fay-Cooper, *The Peoples of Malaysia*, Princeton, N.J.: D. Van Nostrand Co., Inc., 1945.

Dean, Vera Micheles, *The Nature of the Non-Western World*, New York: New American Library of World Literature, Inc., 1957.

Eggan, Fred, ed., *Social Anthropology of North American Tribes*, 2nd. ed., Chicago University of Chicago Press, 1955.

Forde, C. Daryll, *African Worlds: Studies in the Cosmological Ideas and Social Values of African Peoples*, London: Oxford University Press, 1954.

Ginsburg, Norton S., ed., *The Pattern of Asia*, Englewood Cliffs, N.J.: Prentice-Hall, Inc., 1958.

Hsu, Francis L. K., *Americans and Chinese: Two Ways of Life*, New York: Abelard-Schuman, Limited, 1953.

Japanese National Commission for UNESCO, compiler, *Japan, Its Land, People and Culture*, Tokyo: Japanese Government Printing Bureau, 1958.

Linton, Ralph, ed., *Most of the World*, New York: Columbia University Press, 1949.

Maraini, Fosco, *Meeting with Japan*, trans. by Eric Mosbacher, New York: The Viking Press, Inc., 1959.

Martin, Paul S. and G. I. Quimby and D. Collier: *Indians Before Columbus*, Chicago: University of Chicago Press, 1947.

Osgood, Cornelius, *The Koreans and their Culture*, New York: The Ronald Press Company, 1951.

Ottenberg, Simon and Phoebe, *Cultures and Societies of Africa*, New York: Random House, Inc., 1960.

Radcliffe-Brown, A. R. and Daryll Forde, eds., *African Systems of Kinship and Marriage*, London: Oxford University Press, 1950.

Steward, Julian and Louis C. Faron, *Native Peoples of South America*, New York: McGraw-Hill Book Co., Inc., 1959.

Wallbank, T. Walter, *A Short History of India and Pakistan*, New York: New American Library of World Literature, Inc., 1958.

Wright, Arthur F., *Studies in Chinese Thought*, Chicago: University of Chicago Press, 1953.

2. *Monographs on Tribal Groups*

(Where the tribe is not adequately identified in the title the name or location is given in parentheses.)

Africa

Evans-Pritchard, E. E., *Witchcraft, Oracles and Magic Among the Azande*, Oxford: Clarendon Press, 1937.

———, *The Nuer*, Oxford: Clarendon Press, 1940.

———, *Nuer Religion*, Oxford: Clarendon Press, 1956.

Herskovits, Melville J., *Dahomey—An Ancient West African Kingdom*, New York: J. J. Augustin, Inc., Publisher, 1938, 2 vols.

Junod, Henri A., *The Life of a South African Tribe* (Thonga), Neuchatel, Switzerland: Imprimerie Attinger Freres, 1912, 2 vols.

Krige, E. Jensen and J. D., *The Realm of a Rain Queen: A Study of the Pattern of Lovedu Society*, New York: Oxford University Press, 1943.

Nadel, S. F., *Nupe Religion*, London: Routledge and Kegan Paul, Ltd., 1954.

Peristiany, J. G., *The Social Institutions of the Kipsigis*, London: Routledge and Kegan Paul, Ltd., 1939.

Rattray, Robert R., *The Ashanti*, Oxford: Clarendon Press, 1923.

———, *Religion and Art in Ashanti*, Oxford: Clarendon Press, 1927.

Raum, O. F., *Chaga Childhood*, London Oxford University Press, 1940.

Read, Margaret, *Children of their Fathers—Growing up Among the Ngoni of Nyasaland*, New Haven: Yale University Press, 1960.

Richards, Audrey I., *Land, Labor and Diet in Northern Rhodesia* (Bemba), London: Oxford University Press, 1939.

Schapera, Isaac, *The Khoisan People of South Africa* (Bushman and Hottentot), London: Routledge and Kegan Paul, Ltd., 1930.

Wilson, Monica Hunter, *Good Company—A Study of Nyakyusa Age Villages*, London: Oxford University Press, 1951.

The Americas (Indians and Eskimo)

Dennis, Wayne, *The Hopi Child*, New York: Appleton-Century-Crofts, Inc., 1940.

Kluckhohn, Clyde and Dorothea Leighton, *The Navaho*, Cambridge, Mass.: Harvard University Press, 1946.

Leighton, Dorothea and Clyde Kluckhohn, *Children of the People*, (Navaho), Cambridge, Mass.: Harvard University Press, 1947.

Lowie, Robert H., *The Crow Indians*, New York: Farrar, Straus & Cudahy, Inc., 1935.

Opler, Morris Z., *An Apache Life Way,* Chicago: University of Chicago Press, 1941.

Spencer, Robert F., *The North Alaskan Eskimo,* Washington, D.C.: Smithsonian Institution Bureau of American Ethnology, Bulletin 171, 1959.

Thompson, Laura and Alice Joseph, *The Hopi Way,* Chicago: University of Chicago Press, 1945.

India

Majumdar, Dhirendra Nath, *The Affairs of A Tribe* (Hos), Lucknow, India: Universal Publishers Ltd., 1950.

Verrier, Elwin, *The Baiga,* London: John Murray, 1939.

The Pacific

Barton, R. F., *The Kalingas* (Philippines), Chicago: The University of Chicago Press, 1949.

Firth, Raymond, *We, the Tikopia* (Polynesia), New York: American Book Company, 1936.

Fortune, R. F., *Sorcerers of Dobu* (Melanesia), London: Routledge and Kegan Paul, Ltd., 1932.

Hogbin, H. Ian, *Law and Order in Polynesia* (Ontong Java), New York: Harcourt, Brace & World, Inc., 1934.

Malinowski, Bronislaw, *Sexual Life of Savages in Northwestern Melanesia* (Trobriands), New York: Liveright Publishing Corp., 1929.

Mead, Margaret, *Coming of Age in Samoa* (Polynesia), New York: William Morrow & Co., Inc., 1928.

———, *Growing Up in New Guinea* (Manus), New York: William Morrow & Co., Inc., 1930.

———, *New Lives for Old—Cultural Transformation—Manus, 1928-1953,* New York: William Morrow & Co., Inc., 1956.

Quain, Buell, *Fijian Village* (Nakaroka), Chicago: University of Chicago Press, 1948.

Radcliffe-Brown, A. R., *The Andaman Islanders,* Cambridge: Cambridge University Press, 1933.

Spencer, Baldwin and F. J. Gillen, *The Native Tribes of Central Australia* (Arunta), London: Macmillan and Co. Limited, 1899.

Whiting, John W. M., *Becoming a Kwoma—Teaching and Learning in a New Guinea Tribe,* New Haven: Yale University Press, 1941.